of the *at -ing* and *on -ing* patterns here that *being* follows *work at* considerably more often than it follows *work on*: the COHA data contains altogether 32 instances of *work at being*, while *work on being* is found only four times. This would support the observation made earlier of the *at -ing* pattern being associated with more specific, circumscribed, and momentary actions and processes. Although one might then assume that the gerund *becoming* might, in contrast, be more common with *work on -ing*, *work at becoming* and *work on becoming* are roughly equally common in COHA (with only five and four tokens, respectively). Here it is likely that the preference for the *on -ing* pattern as a reflection of its closer association with broader, long-term efforts is not very prominent because the same idea is more idiomatically expressed with the *to-*infinitive (i.e. *work to become*).

Many tokens in the data also include the adverb *hard* modifying the matrix verb, and occurrences of elements of this type could be examined to see whether they are at all indicative of underlying semantic differences between the two constructions. In COHA, different types of adverbials (e.g. of duration or manner) are found with both *work at -ing* and *work on -ing*, and it is mainly the adverb *hard* that shows notable differences between its use with the two constructions. In the data from the period of 1990–2009 in COHA, *hard* was used 40 times with *work at -ing*, whereas it was found only five times with *work on -ing*. Considering that the total numbers of tokens of the two patterns in this period were 83 and 123, respectively, the more frequent use of *hard* with *work at -ing* may indeed be reflective of how the meanings of the two constructions are perceived. While the use of the adverb *hard* is by no means impossible with *work on -ing*, it is perhaps logical to assume that observations on the intensity of efforts are generally more likely to be made on single actions than on actions or projects that take more time.

Some interesting observations can also be made on the adverbial expressions occurring between the matrix verb and the *at/on -ing* complement particularly in the Hansard Corpus data. In general it would seem that Parliamentary speeches allow for greater complexity as regards sentence structure, and instances with six words between the matrix verb and the complement were not rare in the data, as in "I have asked her to work particularly hard in the next year on getting more maintenance paid" (Hansard Corpus, House of Commons, June 20, 1997). A notable difference between the *at -ing* and *on -ing* patterns in the data can be seen in that prepositional phrases headed by *with*, denoting an external party with which the action is jointly performed, are found exclusively with tokens of the *on -ing* pattern. Examples (20a–b) are good illustrations of such tokens:

(20) a. We shall be working closely with the Local Government Association on developing a concordat for central/local relations: [...] (Hansard, House of Lords, July 23, 1997)
   b. The Bill takes forward the Government's commitment that the Inland Revenue will work with employers' representatives and others on reducing technical differences between the administration of tax and national insurance: [...] (Hansard, House of Commons, Jan. 6, 2004)

In the entire Hansard Corpus, there were altogether 67 instances of this type of *with* + NP sequences found between *work* and the *on -ing* complement—most of them in the last 20 years of the corpus data—but no corresponding tokens with the *at -ing* pattern. This difference may be another reflection of the *on -ing* pattern suggesting more concerted and goal-oriented actions.

In addition to examining the lower-level verbs and adverbs used with the *work at -ing* and *work on -ing* patterns, manual inspection of the corpus data prompted a look into whether the tenses and aspects of the matrix verb *work* themselves show differences between the two complement patterns. Tables 2.3 and 2.4 below include the numbers of instances of

Table 2.3 The different forms of the matrix verb *work* when followed by *at/on -ing* in the British National Corpus

	work at -ing		work on -ing	
	Simple	*Progressive*	*Simple*	*Progressive*
Finite				
Present	17	3	11	17
Past	15	2	18	1
Present perfect	5	3	9	9
Past perfect	3	1	–	–
Auxiliary + base	9	–	7	1
Total	**49**	**9**	**45**	**28**
Non-finite				
to-infinitive	31		31	
Gerund	6		11	

Table 2.4 The different forms of the matrix verb *work* when followed by *at/on -ing* in the 2000–2009 section of the COHA corpus

	work at -ing		work on -ing	
	Simple	*Progressive*	*Simple*	*Progressive*
Finite				
Present	13	1	8	19
Past	20	–	9	5
Present perfect	1	–	3	2
Past perfect	1	–	1	1
Auxiliary + base	3	–	7	1
Total	**38**	**1**	**28**	**28**
Non-finite				
to-infinitive	8		13	
Gerund	3		2	

different forms of *work* when followed by *at -ing* and *on -ing* in the BNC and the 2000–2009 data of COHA, respectively:

Based on the findings in Tables 2.3 and 2.4, it appears that the aspectual uses of the matrix verb *work* can be regarded as distinguishing between the *work at -ing* and *work on -ing* constructions, at least to some extent. While both constructions are found with simple (or non-progressive) forms, tokens of *work on -ing* have the matrix verb occurring proportionally more often in the progressive. In the COHA data, the division is clear, with only one instance found of the progressive use of *work* followed by an *at -ing* complement. A simple Chi Square test of the total numbers of the simple and progressive forms of the matrix verbs shows statistical significance for the division in this respect in both British and American English: with the BNC data, the Yates Chi Square for the figures in bold of the two patterns in Table 2.3 is 7.23 and the result is significant ($p < 0.01$), and with the COHA data, the corresponding Yates Chi Square for the figures in bold in Table 2.4 is 22.21 and the result is significant ($p < 0.0001$).

These findings provide further support for the observations made earlier. The use of the progressive forms (such as *is/was working, has/have/had been working*, and auxiliary + *be/have been working*), as observed e.g. by Huddleston (1988, 74), is associated with situations in progress, whereas the simple or non-progressive constructions (e.g., *worked*) "can be used for both static and dynamic situations", but the situation is nevertheless "presented in its totality." Furthermore, in their analysis of the

occurrence of simple and progressive forms of different verbs, Biber et al. (1999, 473) note that "verbs that rarely occur in the progressive fall into two main groups: (a) those that refer to an action that is immediate, and (b) those that refer to a state that is not normally a continuing process." They also observe a connection between the duration of the action and the low frequency of the use of the verbs in the progressive, saying that with dynamic verbs such as *shut, smash, and throw*, "[b]ecause these actions have virtually no duration, such verbs rarely occur in the progressive" (Biber et al. 1999, 474). While the verb *work* is obviously a dynamic verb when it is followed by either an *at -ing* or *on -ing* complement, one could suggest that the fact that *work* occurs more frequently in the progressive when followed by *on -ing* reflects a semantic difference between the two constructions. Compared to *work at -ing*, *work on -ing* could be seen as being more closely associated with the idea of improvement and with actions that are not momentary, but which require at least some time to complete. This observation in turn is in line with the ideas proposed earlier that the senses of the two constructions are influenced by the fundamental meanings of the two prepositions.

2.5   Concluding Remarks

Trying to distinguish between the constructions *work at -ing* and *work on -ing* is arguably a challenging task, even with the help of corpus data. It is therefore perhaps not surprising that dictionaries do not clearly differentiate between the two, while some signs are visible that suggest a difference in their use. One reason for this may be the fact that the major changes in the overall frequencies of the two patterns have not occurred until relatively recently, both in American and British English. In addition, there appears to be some overlap in the uses of the two constructions. However, as has been observed in the qualitative and quantitative analyses of the corpus data, some lines of distinction can be detected as well, and the findings lend support to Bolinger's view of a difference in form coinciding with a difference in meaning. It is worth considering that it is, in fact, the fundamental meanings of the prepositions *at* and *on* which are reflected in the uses of *work at -ing* and *work on -ing*. Overall, *work at -ing* seems to be preferred when referring to actions which are more specific and circumscribed, and the difference between the two constructions in terms of duration of the process is reflected in the occurrences of simple and progressive forms of the matrix verbs. As for the *work on -ing* construction, its frequency appears to be on the rise in both American and British English

in very recent decades, and this study also brought to light a rather special use of the construction where it carries a reactive meaning. Further, more in-depth examination is nevertheless warranted on the matter, which serves as a case study on the nuances that ultimately can be observed in the use of alternative constructions. Some possibilities of examining the issue in more detail could be found, for example, in the study of the two constructions in different text types as well as in the diachronic study of the aspectual uses of the matrix verbs.

REFERENCES

Biber, Douglas, Stig Johansson, Geoffrey Leech, Susan Conrad, and Edward Finegan. 1999. *Longman Grammar of Spoken and Written English*. Harlow: Pearson Education Limited.

Bolinger, Dwight. 1968. Entailment and the Meaning of Structures. *Glossa* 2: 119–127.

Chomsky, Noam. 1986. *Knowledge of Language: Nature, Origin, and Use*. New York: Praeger.

Herskovits, Annette. 1986. *Language and Spatial Cognition. An Interdisciplinary Study of the Prepositions in English*. Cambridge: Cambridge University Press.

Huddleston, Rodney. 1988. *English Grammar: An Outline*. Cambridge: Cambridge University Press.

Rohdenburg, Günter. 2006. The Role of Functional Constraints in the Evolution of the English Complementation System. In *Syntax, Style and Grammatical Norms: English from 1500–2000*, ed. Christine Dalton-Puffer, Dieter Kastovsky, Nicholas Ritt, and Herbert Schendl, 143–166. Bern: Peter Lang.

Rundell, Michael, ed. 2002. *Macmillan English Dictionary for Advanced Learners*. Oxford: Macmillan Publishers.

Schibsbye, Knud. 1970. *A Modern English Grammar with an Appendix on Semantically Related Prepositions*. London: Oxford University Press.

Sinclair, John, ed. 1987. *Collins COBUILD English Language Dictionary*. London: HarperCollins Publishers.

Summers, Della, et al., eds. 2003. *Longman Dictionary of Contemporary English*. 4th ed. Harlow: Longman.

The Oxford English Dictionary (OED Online). 2015. Oxford: Oxford University Press. http://www.oed.com.

Tyler, Andrea, and Vyvyan Evans. 2003. *The Semantics of English Prepositions: Spatial Scenes, Cognition and the Experiential Basis of Meaning*. New York and Cambridge: Cambridge University Press.

Vosberg, Uwe. 2009. Non-Finite Complements. In *One Language, Two Grammars? Differences Between British and American English*, ed. Günter Rohdenburg and Julia Schlüter, 212–227. Cambridge: Cambridge University Press. https://doi.org/10.1017/CBO9780511551970.012.

CHAPTER 3

Semantic Roles and Complement Selection: A Case Study on the Matrix Adjective *Frightened*

Abstract This chapter is a contribution to the study of complement variation of head words, examining the variation between two non-finite sentential complements selected by the adjective *frightened*. The adjective is nowadays found to select *to* infinitive complements and *of -ing* complements, and based on evidence from large electronic corpora, the chapter provides a survey into the diachronic developments in the uses of the two patterns from early nineteenth century to the present day. In addition to the observation of the incidence of variation, the chapter examines syntactic and semantic factors which may play a role in the choice of the complement pattern in both American and British English. Earlier work contains valuable insights, but the present chapter develops a new approach on the basis of the semantic role of the lower subject. In particular, it is proposed that agentive lower subjects are associated with *to* infinitive complements. The relevance of the recently formulated Choice Principle in this regard is considered in relation to the selection properties of the adjective *frightened*, and it is observed that the effect of these semantic features on the choice of the two patterns is of statistical significance in the corpus data analyzed.

Keywords Adjective complementation • Understood subjects • Subject control • Diachronic change • Corpus linguistics

© The Author(s) 2019   37
M. Kaunisto, J. Rudanko, *Variation in Non-finite Constructions in English*, https://doi.org/10.1007/978-3-030-19044-6_3

3.1   Introduction

A central research task in the study of complementation concerns the question of how heads—verbs, adjectives, nouns—can be matched with certain types of complements and what generalizations can be made to characterize the matching in question. The matching problem is especially acute when a head selects more than one type of complement. The present chapter aims to contribute to this area of research by investigating the complement selection properties of the adjective *frightened* as a case study of a predicate selecting more than one type of complement, in order to shed light on the matching problem in recent English.

Consider the sentences in (1a) and (1b), from COHA, the Corpus of Historical American English:

(1) a. The pain had almost gone, but he was frightened to get out of bed in case that dreadful pain came roaring back. (COHA, 1998, FIC)
   b. They are all frightened of taking responsibility for the boy. (COHA, 1993, FIC)

In (1a) and (1b) the matrix predicate is the adjective *frightened*, and it selects a non-finite sentential complement in each of them. In (1a) the complement is a *to* infinitive and in (1b) it is a prepositional gerund of the *of -ing* type, consisting of the preposition *of* and a following *-ing* constituent. It is assumed here that in each case the non-finite complement is sentential, with its own understood or covert subject. This assumption was made by major traditional grammarians, including Jespersen ([1940] 1961, 140), and it is made in much current work. Apart from an appeal to tradition, the sentential status of the complement is supported by the consideration that such an understood subject makes it possible to represent the argument structure of the lower predicate in a straightforward fashion.

As for the matrix predicate in (1a–b), in both sentences the matrix predicate assigns a semantic role to its subject, and both (1a) and (1b) are therefore control constructions. The understood subjects of the lower clauses are then represented by the symbol PRO, an "abstract pronominal element" (Chomsky 1981, 6; see also Davies and Dubinsky 2004, 84).

Assuming the presence of understood subjects in (1a–b), the key parts of these sentences may be represented as in (1a′) and (1b′).

(1) a.´ [[he]$_{NP}$ was [frightened]$_{Adj}$ [[PRO]$_{NP}$ [to]$_{Aux}$ [get out of bed]$_{VP}$]$_{S2}$]$_{S1}$

b.´ [[they]$_{NP}$ are all [frightened]$_{Adj}$ [[of]$_{Prep}$ [[[PRO]$_{NP}$ [taking responsibility for the boy]$_{VP}$]$_{S2}$]$_{NP}$]$_{PP}$]$_{S1}$

One important difference between the structures in (1a´–b´), as outlined in (1a´) and (1b´), concerns the syntactic status of the words *to* and *of* in them. As noted, *of* is a preposition, and (1b´) incorporates the traditional notion of a nominal clause, with the *-ing* clause represented as an NP dominating a sentence. One reason for using the notion of nominal clause is that it makes it possible to keep the simple phrase structure rule for prepositional phrases, which rewrites a PP as Prep and NP.

As for (1a´) the *to* of the *to* infinitive construction is under the Aux node, in the spirit of the analysis of Chomsky (1981, 16) (Chomsky's Infl node corresponds to the more traditional Aux node used here). Distinguishing infinitival *to* and a prepositional gerund syntactically in this way is supported for instance by VP Deletion. As Radford (1997, 53) has pointed out, this rule may apply in the case of a *to* infinitive complement, but it may be noted here that it is excluded in the case of an *of* -*ing* complement. There is thus a contrast in well-formedness between the invented sentences in (2a–b), where (2a) has been modified from (1a) and (2b) has been modified from (1b).

(2) a. He was frightened to get out of bed, but she was not frightened to.

b. *They were frightened of taking responsibility for the boy, but we were not frightened of.

VP Deletion, or its interpretive analogue, is possible in a structure of the type of (1a´) because what follows the word *to* is a VP in (1a´). By contrast, since *of* is a preposition in (1b), it is not followed by a VP, which accounts for the ill-formedness of a sentence of the type of (2b).

In view of the VP Deletion argument, it is clear that the syntactic structures of the sentential complements in (1a–b) are very different. However, it is easy to find *to* infinitive and *of* -*ing* complements of the adjective *frightened* side by side in standard dictionaries. For instance, the *OALD* (2005) lists the complements ~ (**of sth/of doing sth**) | ~ (**to do sth**) | ~ (**that …**), all with the gloss "afraid; feeling fear." *Of* NP and *that* clause complements are here set aside for a later treatment, but as far as *to* infinitives and *of -ing* complements are concerned, the *OALD* (2005) analysis suggests that they are felt to be close in meaning when selected by the adjective *frightened*. It is therefore of interest to investigate them together, taking into account Bolinger's statement—often called Bolinger's Generalization—that a "difference in syntactic form always spells a difference in meaning" (Bolinger 1968, 127).

A first aim of this study is to provide information on the incidence of the two constructions in the last two centuries. This is done on the basis of COHA, the Corpus of Historical American English, and as regards diachronic developments in British English, the Hansard Corpus, is examined.

Another objective is to compare the two constructions in current English, using COCA, the Corpus of Contemporary American English, as the main source of evidence. British English is also investigated in a later section on the basis of the BNC, mainly to compare that core variety with findings on American English based on COCA. A syntactic factor bearing on complement selection is mentioned, but the emphasis is on teasing the two patterns apart from a semantic point of view. The main perspective in the comparison concerns the Choice Principle as a potential factor that might be used to explain the variation in question. The principle has been put forward in very recent work on sentential complementation, but its status cannot be regarded as established as yet. The principle postulates a connection between semantic roles and complement selection. It has been formulated in the following way:

The Choice Principle

In the case of infinitival and gerundial complement options at a time of considerable variation between the two patterns, the infinitive tends to be associated with [+Choice] contexts and the gerund with [−Choice] contexts. (Rudanko 2017, 20)

The concepts of [+Choice] and [−Choice] contexts are developed and illustrated in Sect. 3.3, but to put it briefly, a [+Choice] context is an agentive context and [−Choice] context is a non-agentive context. The study examines whether the Choice Principle can shed light on complement selection in the case of the matrix predicate *frightened*.

3.2 *To* INFINITIVE AND *OF -ING* COMPLEMENTS OF THE ADJECTIVE *FRIGHTENED* IN AMERICAN AND BRITISH ENGLISH IN THE LAST TWO CENTURIES

To shed light on the incidence of *to* infinitive and *of -ing* complements of the adjective *frightened* in the last two centuries, COHA and the Hansard Corpus are consulted here. COHA was chosen because of its size and balanced content as a diachronic corpus, and the large Hansard Corpus, containing transcriptions of speeches in the British Parliament, with its numerous tokens provides us with an insight into the historical shifts in the use of the constructions. The basic search strings used were "frightened to [v?i*]" and "frightened of [v?g*]." These were supplemented with search strings allowing one or two words between *frightened* and *to/of* and with search strings allowing one word between *to/of* and the following infinitive or gerund. The huge majority of relevant tokens were retrieved with the basic search strings, with sentences (3a–d) and (4a–d) being examples, but there were some additional tokens that were retrieved with the supplementary search strings, as in (5a–d).

(3) a. I come from a stock that never would be frightened to show their face to a king, let alone an old noodles that calls himself a jolly-jist. (COHA, 1886, FIC)

    b. I confess I was alarmed and frightened to hear one sentence in the speech which the right hon: Gentleman the Prime Minister made the other night […] (Hansard, House of Commons, Apr. 15, 1886)

    c. Charlie whispered the words as though he were frightened to utter them. (COHA, 2009, FIC)

    d. The national patient safety agency will not work if people are frightened to report things that have gone wrong […] (Hansard, House of Commons, Jan. 17, 2002)

(4) a. I am not frightened of standing up against his acting. (COHA, 1938, MAG)

    b. I think an honest man, in discussing a difficult question like this, should not be frightened of making observations which are received with that kind of derision by hon: Members opposite which indicates that in their judgment he has said something which, from a party point of view, he had better not have said […] (Hansard, House of Commons, Oct. 28, 1912)

    c. Chadfallow often appeared frightened of being seen with Pazel. (COHA, 2008, FIC)

    d. I say one other word about this because we on these Benches are not frightened of mentioning the euro [...] (Hansard, House of Commons, Mar. 17, 2000)

(5) a. He pleased himself all the way home with the anticipation of his wife's smiles and welcome, and he was a little frightened not to see her face at the window the moment his cab arrived. (COHA, 1893, FIC)

    b. [...] while many union members may not approve of a strike, they are frightened not to put up their hands to vote for strike action [...] (Hansard, House of Lords, July 13, 1982)

    c. I'm frightened shitless of being out there on the end of a rubber tube and a couple of wires. (COHA, 1977, FIC)

    d. They are frightened of a policeman: They are frightened in court of facing what is perhaps generally regarded as a clever lawyer who will tie them into knots [...] (Hansard, House of Lords, May 23, 1994)

The search strings also retrieve a large number of tokens that are set aside as irrelevant. Consider the examples in (6a–d).

(6) a. Clara was too much frightened to reason at all about the matter. (COHA, 1869, FIC)

    b. Bryce went down by the pond since I was too frightened to look there. (COHA, 1988, FIC)

    c. Might be waiting upstairs after hearing him come in; might be frightened enough to come down armed with a weapon. (COHA, 1979, FIC)

    d. And it frightened him to know, as he did now, that such a thing can happen to a man. (COHA, 1959, FIC)

In (6a–c) the infinitival complement is linked to a modifier of the higher adjective (see Quirk et al. 1985, 1140–42; Huddleston and Pullum 2002, 546), and may be termed an indirect complement. Such indirect complements are very common with the adjective *frightened*, but this study concentrates on complements of the adjectival head, and indirect complements are set aside. As for (6d), searches allowing for words between *frightened*

Table 3.1 The incidence of *to* infinitival and *of -ing* complements of the adjective *frightened* in the period from the 1810s to the 2000s in COHA

Decade	Size (million words)	to infinitives (pmw)	of -ing (pmw)
1810s	1.2	1 (0.8)	0
1820s	6.9	1 (0.1)	0
1830s	13.8	1 (0.1)	0
1840s	16.0	3 (0.2)	0
1850s	16.5	3 (0.2)	0
1860s	17.1	2 (0.1)	0
1870s	18.6	2 (0.1)	0
1880s	20.3	6 (0.3)	0
1890s	20.6	5 (0.2)	0
1900s	22.1	5 (0.2)	0
1910s	22.7	4 (0.2)	0
1920s	25.7	6 (0.2)	0
1930s	24.6	4 (0.2)	2 (0.1)
1940s	24.3	2 (0.1)	0
1950s	24.5	4 (0.2)	1 (0.0)
1960s	24.0	9 (0.4)	6 (0.3)
1970s	23.8	3 (0.1)	3 (0.1)
1980s	25.3	9 (0.4)	4 (0.2)
1990s	27.9	12 (0.4)	8 (0.3)
2000s	29.6	6 (0.2)	4 (0.1)

and the following *of -ing* complement also bring up verbal uses of *frightened*, which should of course be excluded.

Table 3.1 gives information about the frequencies of the two types of non-finite complements of the adjective *frightened* in COHA. The normalized frequencies (per million words) are given in parentheses.

The figures in Table 3.1 are of interest for a number of reasons. They reveal that as far as the nineteenth century is concerned, some tokens of *to* infinitival complements were found in most decades, but the *of -ing* pattern was apparently absent from the material in that century. More plentiful tokens of both patterns tend to be found in the twentieth century, especially in the 1960s and from the 1980s onwards, with the *to* infinitive still tending to be more frequent than the *of -ing* pattern.

As regards the occurrences of the two constructions in the speeches given in the British Parliament in the last two centuries, the corresponding figures are presented in Table 3.2, and illustrated in Fig. 3.1.

Table 3.2   The incidence of *to* infinitival and *of -ing* complements of the adjective *frightened* in the period from the 1810s to the 2000s in the Hansard Corpus

Decade	Size (million words)	to *infinitives (pmw)*	of -ing *(pmw)*
1860s	34.2	–	1 (0.0)
1870s	37.1	–	–
1880s	60.0	2 (0.0)	–
1890s	51.2	–	–
1900s	64.7	4 (0.1)	3 (0.0)
1910s	79.8	10 (0.1)	8 (0.1)
1920s	71.7	16 (0.2)	14 (0.2)
1930s	95.2	23 (0.2)	30 (0.3)
1940s	94.8	37 (0.4)	42 (0.4)
1950s	121.0	50 (0.4)	63 (0.5)
1960s	152.0	101 (0.7)	128 (0.8)
1970s	163.3	122 (0.7)	106 (0.6)
1980s	183.7	190 (1.0)	132 (0.7)
1990s	177.1	215 (1.2)	131 (0.7)
2000–05	88.4	74 (0.8)	66 (0.7)

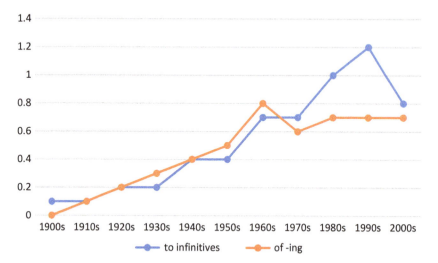

Fig. 3.1   The normalized frequencies *to* infinitival and *of -ing* complements of the adjective *frightened* from the 1900s to the 2000s in the Hansard Corpus

As can be seen in Table 3.2 and Fig. 3.1, in the British English data the two constructions are rare in the nineteenth century, followed by a steady increase in frequency of both patterns during the twentieth century. Over four decades, from the 1930s to the 1960s, the *of -ing* pattern even outnumbered the *to* infinitives slightly, but the *to* infinitives have been more frequent since the 1970s. In the speeches in the 2000s, the normalized frequencies show a decline of both patterns, with *to* infinitives still being more frequent than the *of -ing* pattern. Considering the most recent data in COHA and Hansard in this respect, the results are similar to each other as to the proportions between the two constructions, although in the 2000–05 data in Hansard, the *of -ing* pattern is perhaps showing signs of strengthening. It is also perhaps worth noting that both patterns are generally more frequent in the Parliamentary debates than in COHA, as seen in the normalized frequencies of the patterns. This probably has to do with the nature of the Parliamentary debates themselves: as the members are discussing current problems and laws that are being drafted, different kinds of concerns are described explicitly with the use of the adjective *frightened*.

In comparing the two patterns more closely, it is expedient to concentrate on data from very recent English, where the *of -ing* pattern has apparently come to be a potential competitor of the *to* infinitival pattern, as evidenced by the findings in the diachronic data. Such closer analyses are presented in the following section.

3.3 *To* INFINITIVE AND *OF -ING* COMPLEMENTS OF THE ADJECTIVE *FRIGHTENED* IN COCA

COCA, the Corpus of Contemporary American English, offers data from very recent English, and suggests itself as a database in the closer analysis of the two patterns, also taking its balanced nature and its size into account. The same search strings as above were used to study the adjective *frightened* in the corpus. A large number of irrelevant tokens were again encountered, and these were overwhelmingly of the same types as those illustrated in (6a–d) above, with examples of the type "*too frightened to* Verb" being especially common, as in the COHA data. Still, the investigator also needs to be alert to other types of irrelevant tokens, as for instance in (7), from the spoken medium, where the *to* infinitive is an adjunct, in the nature of a fixed phrase, not a complement of *frightened*.

(7) Unidentified Woman 1: I was frightened to begin with. Something total out of reality, it felt like. (COCA, 2008, SPOK)

The present investigators have counted 193 potentially relevant tokens in the COCA data, made up from 124 *to* infinitives and 69 *of*-*ing* complements. These figures confirm the overall finding, suggested by the data from COHA, that *to* infinitives are still more frequent than *of*-*ing* complements with *frightened* in recent English. An initial illustration of each from COCA is given in (8a–b).

(8) a. A local journalist, frightened to give his name, said by phone that he had witnessed minor violence between Nahda supporters and other voters in Jendouba, a city south of Tunis. (COCA, 2011, NEWS)

b. Doctors will remain frightened of making positive decisions because of ancient laws which bear little relationship to modern high-tech medicine. (COCA, 1990, NEWS)

Turning to the task of considering explanatory factors bearing on variation between the two complements, the Extraction Principle should be mentioned first. It is a non-semantic principle that has come to be widely accepted as a relevant factor in the complement choice between *to* infinitives and gerunds, following pioneering work by Rohdenburg (2006) and Vosberg (2003a, b, 2006). Vosberg has provided a clear formulation of the principle.

The Extraction Principle

In the case of infinitival or gerundial complement options, the infinitive will tend to be favored in environments where a complement of the subordinate clause is extracted (by topicalization, relativization, comparativization, or interrogation, etc.) and crosses clause boundaries. (Vosberg 2003a, 308)[1]

In other work it has been noted that extraction rules may also move adjuncts in addition to complements (see Vosberg 2006; Rudanko 2006), and this broader view is adopted here. In the present dataset there are altogether nine extractions that come within the scope of the Extraction Principle. Two examples are given in (9a–b), both representing Relativization, which is the most frequent extraction rule in the data.

(9) a. This is the story of my attempt to share my passion for astronomy with a community of individuals that society is largely unaware of and is perhaps a little frightened to acknowledge. (COCA, 2002, ACAD)
   b. This is why the idea of surrender is so interesting to me, because surrendering is what we are most frightened of doing. (COCA, 2013, MAG)

In view of the Extraction Principle, the expectation is that extraction contexts would tend to favour *to* infinitives. For what it is worth, seven of the nine tokens do involve *to* infinitives, as in (9a), and besides the token given in (9b) there is only one other example of an *of -ing* complement in an extraction environment, as defined by the principle. The finding is broadly in accordance with the Extraction Principle, but the low number of extractions means that there is ample scope for additional work on factors influencing variation in the present material. The rest of this study is devoted to this research task. Because the status of the Extraction Principle in explaining variation between *to* infinitives and gerunds can be taken for granted on the basis of earlier work, the nine tokens with extractions in the present material are excluded from further consideration here. This leaves 117 *to* infinitives and 67 *of -ing* complements to be considered.

The main focus is on the Choice Principle, which is a semantic principle,[2] but as a preliminary it is of interest briefly to mention one earlier approach to the task of comparing *to* infinitives and gerunds from a semantic perspective, that of Allerton (1988). He identifies several features to sum up the "infinitive-gerund distinction, in its healthy state." These are listed in Table 3.3.

The features listed by Allerton are not always applicable to separate the two patterns. For instance, to consider the specific subject versus non-specific subject dichotomy, in the case of the adjective *frightened* both types of complements involve straightforward subject control, as is for instance clear in the case in (1a–b) and (8a–b), where both lower subjects are controlled by the higher subjects. However, the features identified by Allerton are worth keeping in mind when comparing the semantics of infinitives and gerunds.

For its part, the Choice Principle does not seek to render nugatory the types of features and properties identified by Allerton and others, but the new principle is based on the potential relevance of semantic roles to complement selection, and it was developed independently of the types of

Table 3.3 Allerton's view of features relevant to the infinitive-gerund distinction

Infinitive	Gerund
Infrequent activity	Regular activity
Intermittent activity	Continuous activity
Interrupted activity	Continuing activity
Uncompleted activity	Completed activity
Contingent/possible event	Event presented factually
Particular time and place	Neutral time and place
Specific subject	Non-specific subject
More verbal character	More nominal character

Source: Allerton (1988, 21)

properties identified in earlier work. As stated above, the principle has to do with the agentivity or otherwise of the lower (understood) subject in the sentential complement of a higher predicate, and agentive subjects are marked as [+Choice] and non-agentive ones as [−Choice]. The term is here also applied to the predicate of the lower clause, which assigns a semantic role to the subject in question. That predicate is agentive if its subject is an Agent. Otherwise it is non-agentive.

A full survey of earlier work on the notion of an Agent cannot be attempted here, but some comments on it are in order. A helpful point of departure is provided by Gruber's comment that "agentive verb is one whose subject refers to an animate object which is thought of as the willful source or agent of the activity described in the sentence" (Gruber 1967, 943). In a later contribution, Jackendoff (1990, 129) listed "three semi-autonomous parts" in his discussion of the Agent: "doer of action," "volitional Actor," and "extrinsic instigator." For his part, Dowty gave prominence to the notion of "volitional involvement in an event or state" in his discussion of what he termed the "Agent Proto-Role" (1991, 582). Here the notion of volitional involvement is viewed as an important feature of agentivity, and it is supplemented with the notions of control and responsibility. That is, an Agent designates an entity that is volitionally involved in an event, activity or state of affairs, has control over it, at least to some degree, and is (or can be held) responsible for it. (The three notions are prominent in Hundt's (2004, 49) discussion of agentivity; for the notion of control, see also Berman (1970).) An agentive subject and the predicate that assigns the reading are then marked as [+Choice], and their non-agentive counterparts are marked as [−Choice].

To illustrate the distinction between [+Choice] and [−Choice] interpretations, consider the examples in (10a–b) and (11a–b), from the present material.

(10) a. Now Nick is frightened to put money in the stock market. (COCA, 2001, SPOK)

   b. At twelve, on an Outward Bound trip, I had listened to Tazewell, red faced and hysterical, cry for a good twenty minutes because he was frightened of riding a chestnut Tennessee Walker down a nature trail. (COCA, 2012, FIC)

(11) a. Her chin juts out like Alana's when she nods yes, as if she's relieved and frightened to have her feelings discovered. (COCA, 2001, FIC)

   b. It was absurd, but Vivienne was frightened of being snubbed; Beth was so warm and outgoing, so friendly and natural with everyone around her, yet Vivienne sensed some evasion, something she did not understand. (COCA, 1995, FIC)

The relevant predicates in (10a–b) are *put money in the stock market* and *riding a chestnut Tennessee Walker down a nature trail* and they are [+Choice] in their sentences. For instance, the predicate *put money in the stock market*, as used in (10a), encodes an event or an action that the referent of the subject is volitionally involved in, has control over and is responsible for. For its part, the predicate *riding a Tennessee Walker down a nature trail*, as used in (10b), is similarly [+Choice].

By contrast, the predicate *have her feelings discovered*, as used in (11a), encodes a situation that the referent of the subject is not volitionally involved in, does not have control over, and cannot be held to be responsible for. As noted in Rudanko (2012), the construction "have NP past participle" can be causative, with a [+Choice] interpretation, as in the likely reading of *He had all the prisoners punished* (see Palmer 1974, 199). However, in (11a) the construction has a non-causative, "happenstance" interpretation, of the type also likely to be relevant in *Alberto Tomba collided with a slalom pole and had his goggles knocked askew* (COCA, 2012, cited in Rudanko 2012). As for (11b), it illustrates a common type of construction that is also prototypically [−Choice]. The lower clause in (11b) is passive in form, and the understood subject of the lower predicate represents, or is derived from, the direct object of the corresponding active, which has the Patient role, the role that may be seen as the opposite of an Agent.

The examples in (10a–b) and (11a–b) can also be used to illustrate another feature of predicates that is of interest from the point of view of the [+/–Choice] distinction. This concerns imperatives. They are of relevance in the present context for a reason well expressed by Taylor:

> Prototypically, an imperative instructs a person to do something, and is therefore only acceptable if a person has a choice between carrying out the instruction or not. (Taylor 2003, 31)

A [+Choice] predicate is then more natural or more likely in an imperative than a [–Choice] predicate. Here the imperative *Put money in the stock market!* may be compared with the imperative *Be snubbed!*, to use the lower predicates of (10a) and (11b). Of these, the former seems more natural than the latter.

The illustrations from the present material in (10a–b) and (11a–b) also show that the Choice Principle cannot be a categorical condition. The *to* infinitive in (10a) goes with a [+Choice] interpretation, but crucially the *to* infinitive of (11a) goes with a [–Choice] interpretation. As for *of -ing* complements, the *of -ing* complement in (11b) is linked to a [–Choice] reading, but that in (10b) is linked to a [+Choice] reading. The two types of complements are therefore flexible enough not to be limited to one type of interpretation only. However, while the Choice Principle, as stated, only predicts a tendency, it is of interest to apply it to the 117 *to* infinitives and 67 *of -ing* complements at hand. The results obtained are given in Table 3.4. Applying the Chi Square test to the findings, the Chi Square is as high as 30.16, and the results are significant at the level of $p < 0.0001$ (df = 1).

The Choice Principle thus receives support from the present data on infinitival and gerundial complements of the adjective *frightened*. The finding is in line with earlier work showing the relevance of the Choice Principle to the complement selection properties of the adjectives *afraid*, *scared*, and *terrified*, discussed in Rickman and Rudanko (2018). Such

Table 3.4   [+Choice] and [–Choice] interpretations of *to* infinitive and *of -ing* complements of the adjective *frightened* in COCA

	[+Choice]	[–Choice]
to infinitives	93	24
of -ing	26	41

adjectives in the relevant usages involving subject control are semantically related in expressing the emotion of fear, and these findings, taken together, suggest that the Choice Principle may bear on the complement selection properties of not only individual adjectives but of classes of adjectives that are semantically related.

In addition, the perspective of the Choice Principle also points to additional lines of investigation. For instance, it is of interest to examine the nature of the 24 *to* infinitives found with *frightened* that are [–Choice]. It is striking that in as many as 11 of them the lower VP is headed by the verb *see*. Two examples are given in (12a–b).

(12) a. Linda bent over to look and was frightened to see the toe turning pink. (COCA, 1997, FIC)
b. I was surprised and a bit frightened to see that I actually liked it. (COCA, 1992, NEWS)

While it is appropriate to regard the lower predicates with the verb *see* embedded under *frightened* in (12a–b) as [–Choice] (see also Gruber 1967 on the non-agentive nature of *see*, as opposed to the agentive nature of *look*), the high frequency of the combination *frightened to see* ... suggests a combination that may be approaching a fixed phrase. Sometimes it may also be possible to view the level of *see* as a bridge between the higher adjective and the complement of *see*, where the intermediate level of *see* is less prominent from a communication point of view than the clause embedded under it. (See Vosberg 2003b for the notion of a bridge.) For instance, if the intermediate *see* level of embedding were omitted in (12b), the resulting sentence *I was surprised and a bit frightened that I actually liked it* is not very different in its communicative content from the content of (12b).

Another point about [–Choice] contexts is also worth making. It was noted above that a passive lower clause provides a typical, or even prototypical, [–Choice] environment, since the lower subject in this case generally represents, or is derived from, the object of the active version of the sentence, with the Patient role, which in a sense is the opposite of an Agent. Three additional examples are given in (13a–c).

(13) a. These young women succumbed to pressure and manipulation from their boyfriends to trade sex because they were desperate, frightened of being beaten up, or both. (COCA, 2006, ACAD)

b. Matt was so frightened of being killed instead that he executed the plan and knocked the two inspectors out. (COCA, 2014, FIC)

c. [...] legislators are often frightened of being blackmailed. (COCA, 1997, ACAD)

The examples in (13a–c) all feature *of -ing* complements for the simple reason that there does not appear to be a single *to* infinitive complement among the 117 *to* infinitives under consideration where the lower clause is in the passive. On the other hand, there are 14 examples of *of -ing* complements with passive lower clauses. In other words, when the lower clause is in the passive, there is a strong tendency for the sentential complement to be of the *of -ing* type. This finding is of interest in confirming the Choice Principle.

It is also of interest to probe the possibility of *to* infinitive complements with passive lower clauses slightly further, going briefly beyond COCA. Such constructions are also very rare in other very large corpora of current English, including in the Corpus of American Soap Operas and in the Corpus of Web-Based English (GloWbE). (For discussion of British English on the basis of the BNC and the most recent segments of Hansard, see Sect. 3.4.) Still the odd example can be found, as in (14), from the New Zealand part of the latter corpus.

(14) In an age when people are frightened to be labelled with the mental health tag this man has put people's attempts to help fight the stigma back a century. (GloWbE-NZ, General: "Nigel Latta's one of them")

An *of -ing* version of sentence (14) is likewise well formed of course, for consider (15), which contains the key part of (14) in a modified form.

(15) ... people are frightened of being labelled with the mental health tag ...

To characterize the difference between the *to* infinitive and *of -ing* constructions in (14) and (15), it may be possible to invoke the [+Choice] associations of *to* infinitives. The complement of *frightened* in [14] is [−Choice], but there may still be a touch of a sense of control or volition in the case of (14), whereas in (15) it is harder to detect a trace of control or volition. It has been observed that *to* infinitive complements in general tend to have the semantic role of Goal in subject control constructions (Rudanko 1989, 35; see also Smith and Escobedo 2001), and the Goal like associations of the *to* infinitive in (14) are in alignment with the element of control or volition in (14), which may also suggest a prospect of an event more likely to happen than in the case of an *of -ing* complement (cf. also Rickman and Rudanko 2018, 64). The reference to "people's attempts to help fight the stigma" later in the sentence is worth noting in this context. By contrast, in (15) the gerundial complement is more Source like, indicating the source of fear, with less suggestion of control or volition. Here it may also be possible to refer to Allerton's (1988, 20) remark that an adjective with a *to* infinitive complement may take on a more abstract meaning, whereas with a prepositional gerund the same adjective keeps its lexical meaning more strictly. Be that as it may, the larger point made on the basis of COCA regarding passive lower clauses remains that in such lower clauses *to* infinitive complements are very rare with the adjective *frightened*, whereas *of -ing* complements are considerably more frequent, and that is accounted for by the Choice Principle.

3.4 *To* Infinitive and *of -ing* Complements of the Adjective *Frightened* in Recent British English

The discussion has so far dealt mainly with American English, but it is appropriate to supplement it with a consideration of the BNC, the British National Corpus, and to compare the results obtained above with the evidence of that corpus, which remains the standard corpus for the study of fairly recent British English. Analytic comments are also appended on the 1990s and 2000s of the Hansard Corpus, to gain information on the most recent usage in a text type of British English. Both types of non-finite complements are of course found in the BNC. The basic search strings— "frightened to [v?i*]," and "frightened of [v?g*]"—produce 156 hits for *to* infinitives, and 84 hits for *of -ing* complements. The latter are all relevant, but among the former there are numerous tokens of indirect complements, of the type *he was too frightened to intervene* (BNC, K1J). When these are set aside, 94 *to* infinitive complements remain. *To* infinitive complements are therefore more frequent than *of -ing* complements with the adjective *frightened* in the BNC, as they were in COCA, but the margin in favour of *to* infinitives is slightly more narrow in the BNC than in COCA. Two initial illustrations are given in (16a–b).

(16) a. I was frightened to go back to the place that had torn me apart.
        (BNC, K32, Newspapers)
     b. He was frightened of touching her. (BNC, GWF, Fiction)

As regards extractions, there are four of them (one of them slightly dubious),[3] with two out of *to* infinitives and two (including the slightly dubious one) out of *of -ing* complements, which is slightly surprising in view of the Extraction Principle, but the numbers are of course much too low to have broader significance. An example of extraction out of an *of -ing* complement is given in (17).

(17) I've nothing more to be frightened of losing. My wife, as I told you, is no longer with us. (BNC, CN3, Fiction)

The four tokens with extraction can again be set aside, because of the established status of the Extraction Principle. This leaves 92 *to* infinitives and 82 *of -ing* complements. When these are considered with respect to the Choice Principle, the results given in Table 3.5 are obtained.

The Chi Square in this case is 30.32, which is slightly lower than in the case of COCA, but the results are still significant at the level of $p < 0.0001$ (df = 1). Examples of [+Choice] and [−Choice] contexts are given in (18a–b) and (19a–b).

(18) a. As he walked on to the first tee he couldn't get any proper words out at all, and so I was frightened to speak to him in case he thought I was teasing him. (BNC, ASA, Miscellaneous)
     b. People are frightened of using their taps, their baths, their toilets because of using water and paying for it. (BNC, HDT, Spoken)
(19) a. I think about it a hell of a lot you know, not with morbid fascination but because everything that I went through gave me inner strength and I am frightened to lose it. (BNC, K5D, Newspapers)

Table 3.5 [+Choice] and [−Choice] interpretations of *to* infinitive and *of -ing* complements of *frightened* in the BNC

	[+Choice]	[−Choice]
to infinitives	87	5
of -ing	48	34

b. Do you think that perhaps in many cases they're frightened of losing their jobs? (BNC, KRT, Broadcast news)

Table 3.5 shows that the Choice Principle has a significant bearing on the complement selection properties of *frightened* in the BNC. A further issue raised by the Choice Principle concerns lower clauses that are passive in form, since these are prototypical [–Choice] contexts. The Choice Principle therefore predicts that they may favour *of -ing* complements as compared to *to* infinitives. There are 12 of them and in ten of them the complement is indeed of the *of -ing* type, and in two it is of the *to* infinitive type. Illustrations are given in (20a–b).

(20) a. Half the class refused to go to the lessons, frightened of being set on fire or being thrown through a window, but Endill liked the suspense of waiting to see what each mixture did next. (BNC, AMB, Fiction)
b. Even now she's frightened to be seen on television for fear of reprisals. (BNC, K22, News script)

The ratio of ten to two in this context is in accordance with the Choice Principle, given the overall preponderance of *to* infinitives over *of -ing* complements in the data. At the same time, the *to* infinitive is not impossible. While the understood subject has the role of Patient or Undergoer, the *to* infinitive still appears to convey some element or tinge of control on the part of the referent of the higher subject, coreferential with the lower subject, in a way reminiscent of the interpretation of sentence (14) above. The presence of the prepositional phrase *for fear of reprisals* in (20b) relates to motivation and goes well with the *to* infinitive.

The BNC has texts from a wide variety of text types but the closing date for selection was 1993, and the corpus is less than ideal for the study of very recent British English. The Hansard Corpus is restricted to parliamentary debates, but it offers a window into usage in that text type in more recent British English, and some comments on the possible salience of the Choice Principle in the 1990s and the first half of the 2000s, up to 2005, may also be offered here. As is clear from Table 3.2, both types of non-finite complements of the adjective *frightened* are fairly frequent during this period, with the total of *to* infinitives being $215 + 74 = 289$ and that of *of -ing* complements being $131 + 66 = 197$. There are four extractions, all of them in the context of *to* infinitives, which is consistent with the Extraction Principle. An example is given in (21).

Table 3.6 [+Choice] and [−Choice] interpretations of *to* infinitive and *of -ing* complements of the adjective *frightened* in the period from 1990 to 2005 in the Hansard Corpus

	[+Choice]	[−Choice]
to infinitives	283	2
of -ing	131	66

(21) The sooner he does so and says what I believe he really feels but is frightened to say at the moment, the sooner we can move ahead in the field. (Hansard, House of Commons, Mar. 8, 1995)

The four extractions, three from the 1990s and one from the 2000s, can be set aside since they come within the purview of the Extraction Principle. Turning to the Choice Principle, Table 3.6 offers information on the interpretations of these tokens with respect to the Choice Principle. The Chi Square in this case is as high as 100.73, and the results are significant at the level of $p < 0.0001$ (df = 1).

Illustrations of [+Choice] contexts are given in (22a–b), and of [−Choice] contexts in (23a–b).

(22) a. Age Concern strongly supports the measure, as many elderly people are frightened to go out after dark: [...] (Hansard, House of Commons, Jan. 19, 1996)
  b. Everyone has been frightened of taking on new ideas and responsibilities [...] (Hansard, House of Lords, Apr. 30, 2003)
(23) a. Not this Prime Minister: He wants to climb, but is frightened to fall: [...] (Hansard, House of Lords, July 11, 2000)
  b. One of the difficulties lies in finding out that bullying is taking place: Police officers are only too well aware that victims or witnesses are frightened of being labelled as grasses or snitches [...] (Hansard, House of Lords, Dec. 13, 2000)

In the present set of data there are as many as 31 tokens where the lower clause is in the passive, as in (23b), which is a prototypical [−Choice] context. In all of them the complement is of the *of -ing* type. This is not to say that a *to* infinitive should necessarily be considered ill formed in this context. On the contrary, it seems quite conceivable to form a *to* infinitive for instance in the case of (23b), as in the invented sentence *Police officers are only too well aware that victims or witnesses are frightened to be labelled as grasses or snitches* and that variant would carry a slightly different shade of meaning compared to (23b), with a tinge of volition, along the lines of interpretations pointed out above, as for instance for sentence (14). Overall, the Choice Principle is supported by the set of Hansard data as an explanatory factor bearing on variation between the two non-finite complements in that data. It is a further benefit of the principle that it also points to the importance to going beyond corpus findings where this can shed further light on the system of English predicate complementation.

3.5 Concluding Remarks

This study showed on the basis of COHA and the Hansard Corpus that *to* infinitive and *of -ing* complements of the adjective *frightened* were very rare in the nineteenth century. What complements there were, were mostly of the *to* infinitive variety. In more recent English, both types of complements were shown to be more frequent, especially from the 1960s onwards. The comparison of the two patterns was therefore conducted on the basis of data from COCA. It was supplemented with a consideration of the BNC to shed light on the two non-finite complements in fairly recent British English.

Sizeable numbers of both complements were found in COCA. The Extraction Principle was considered, but the number of extractions was found to be low with the adjective *frightened*, which reduces the appeal of the principle in the present case. The main interest in the analysis centered on the Choice Principle. It was found to be of statistical significance as a factor bearing on complement choice in both COCA and the BNC, with *to* infinitives linked to [+Choice] contexts and *to -ing* complements linked to [−Choice] contexts, as predicted by the principle. In further discussion of the principle a construction was isolated where the lower clause is in the passive. This exemplifies a prototypical [−Choice] environment, and it was noted that in this context *to* infinitives are rare in both American and British English, as predicted by the Choice Principle. Nevertheless, sometimes tokens of this type are encountered, and it was suggested that the Choice Principle may be helpful even in their interpretation, in that they may carry a tinge of control. The present study naturally invites further work on the possible applicability of the Choice Principle in the case of other matrix predicates selecting to infinitives and gerundial complements introduced by the preposition *of*.

Notes

1. Rohdenburg (2016) is a wide-ranging study of extractions out of sentential complements, and a major conclusion in this article is that the *to* infinitive—Rohdenburg uses the term "marked infinitive"—"enjoys a privileged or target status in extraction contexts" (Rohdenburg 2016, 481) and that the privileged status also holds in relation to gerunds. The present authors take these conclusions to confirm the essence of the Extraction Principle.
2. Discontinuities, as for instance in *Although I am frightened even now to admit it, I surely hoped for this to come to pass* ... (COCA, 1999, FIC), have also been considered as a factor bearing on complement choice between *to* infinitives and gerunds in a number of studies, but it appears on the basis of Rohdenburg (1995, 75) and Vosberg (2006, 63, 175) that insertions are more relevant as a factor when the variation in question is between *to* infinitives and non-prepositional gerunds, and that it is less relevant, or perhaps even not relevant, when comparing *to* infinitives and prepositional gerunds, as in the present case. In the present data, seven *to* infinitives display some type of discontinuity, and the corresponding number in the case of *of -ing* complements is eight. Discontinuities are therefore not excluded from the semantic analysis that follows.
3. The slightly dubious example is ... *I mean what is it they actually, you know, frightened of being rushed into? Mm (pause) I mean* ... (BNC, KDJ, Spoken conversation). The example is conversational English, and it may be slightly fragmented. Assuming that a copula is missing, the example can be included as a token involving extraction.

References

Allerton, David. 1988. 'Infinitivitis' in English. In *Essays on the English Language and Applied Linguistics on the Occasion of Gerhard Nickels 60th Birthday*, ed. J. Klegraf and D. Nehls, 11–23. Heidelberg: Julius Groos Verlag.

Berman, Arlene. 1970. Agent, Experiencer and Controllability. In *Mathematical Linguistics and Automatic Translation*. Report NSF-24, 203–236. Cambridge, MA: Harvard University.

Bolinger, Dwight. 1968. Entailment and the Meaning of Structures. *Glossa* 2: 119–127.

Chomsky, Noam. 1981. *Lectures on Government and Binding*. Dordrecht: Foris.

Davies, William D., and Stanley Dubinsky. 2004. *The Grammar of Raising and Control: A Course in Syntactic Argumentation*. Oxford: Blackwell.

Dowty, David. 1991. Thematic Proto-Roles and Argument Selection. *Language* 67 (3): 547–619.

Gruber, Jeffrey S. 1967. Look and See. *Language* 43 (4): 937–947.

Huddleston, Rodney, and Geoffrey K. Pullum. 2002. *The Cambridge Grammar of the English Language*. Cambridge: Cambridge University Press.

Hundt, Marianne. 2004. Animacy, Agentivity, and the Spread of the Progressive in Modern English. *English Language and Linguistics* 8 (1): 47–69.

Jackendoff, Ray. 1990. *Semantic Structures*. Cambridge, MA: The MIT Press.

Jespersen, Otto. [1940] 1961. *A Modern English Grammar on Historical Principles. Part V: Syntax*. Vol. IV. Reprinted 1961. London and Copenhagen: George Allen and Unwin/Ejnar Munksgaard.

Palmer, Frank R. [1965] 1974. *The English Verb*. 2nd ed. London: Longman.

Quirk, Randolph, Sidney Greenbaum, Geoffrey Leech, and Jan Svartvik. 1985. *A Comprehensive Grammar of the English Language*. London: Longman.

Radford, Andrew. 1997. *Syntactic Theory and the Structure of English. A Minimalist Approach*. Cambridge: Cambridge University Press.

Rickman, Paul, and Juhani Rudanko. 2018. *Corpus-Based Studies on Non-Finite Complements in Recent English*. London: Palgrave Macmillan.

Rohdenburg, Günter. 1995. Betrachtungen zum Auf- und Abstieg einiger Präpositioneller Konstruktionen im Englischen. *North-Western European Language Evolution (NOWELE)* 26: 67–124.

———. 2006. The Role of Functional Constraints in the Evolution of the English Complementation System. In *Syntax, Style and Grammatical Norms: English from 1500–2000*, ed. Christine Dalton-Puffer, Dieter Kastovsky, Nicholas Ritt, and Herbert Schendl, 143–166. Bern: Peter Lang.

———. 2016. Testing Two Principles with Respect to the Extraction of Elements Out of Complement Clauses in English. *English Language and Linguistics* 20 (3): 463–481.

Rudanko, Juhani. 1989. *Complementation and Case Grammar: A Syntactic and Semantic Study of Selected Patterns of Complementation in Present-Day English*. Albany, NY: SUNY Press.

———. 2006. Watching English Grammar Change. *English Language and Linguistics* 10 (1): 31–48.

———. 2012. Exploring Aspects of the Great Complement Shift, with Evidence from the *TIME* Corpus and COCA. In *The Oxford Handbook of the History of English*, ed. Terttu Nevalainen and Elizabeth Traugott, 222–232. Oxford: Oxford University Press.

———. 2017. *Infinitives and Gerunds in Recent English: Studies on Non-Finite Complements in Recent English*. London: Palgrave Macmillan.

Smith, Michael, and Joyce Escobedo. 2001. The Semantics of *to* Infinitival vs. *-ing* Verb Complements in English. In *CLS 37: The Main Session. Proceedings from the Main Session of the Thirty-seventh Meeting of the Chicago Linguistic Society*, ed. M. Andronis, C. Ball, H. Elston, and S. Neuvel, 549–563. Chicago: Chicago Linguistic Society.

Taylor, John R. 2003. Meaning and Context. In *Motivation in Language. Studies in Honor of Günter Radden*, ed. H. Cuyckens, T. Berg, R. Dirven, and K.-U. Panther, 27–48. Amsterdam: John Benjamins.

Vosberg, Uwe. 2003a. The Role of Extractions and *horror aequi* in the Evolution of *-ing* Complements in Modern English. In *Determinants of Grammatical Variation in English*, ed. G. Rohdenburg and B. Mondorf, 305–327. Mouton de Gruyter: Berlin and New York.

———. 2003b. Cognitive Complexity and the Establishment of *-ing* Constructions with Retrospective Verbs in Modern English. In *Insights into Late Modern English*, ed. M. Dossena and C. Jones, 197–220. Bern: Peter Lang.

———. 2006. *Die Grosse Komplementverschiebung*. Tübingen: Narr.

Wehmeier, Sally, Colin McIntosh, and Joanna Turnbull, eds. 2005. *The Oxford Advanced Learner's Dictionary of English*. 7th ed. Oxford: Oxford University Press.

CHAPTER 4

Complement Selection and the Syntactic Status of Infinitival *to*: The Case of the Verb *Submit*

Abstract Trends of change in the system of English predicate are often summed up under the label of the Great Complement Shift. An important aspect of the Shift concerns the increasing spread of gerundial complements at the expense of *to* infinitives. The spread affects *to* infinitives in relation to a number of gerundial constructions, and the present chapter offers a case study dealing with *to* infinitives and what have been called *to* -*ing* complements, selected by the matrix verb *submit*. The chapter examines the incidence of the two patterns with *submit* in both American and British English in the last two centuries, with data from COHA and the Hansard Corpus, which have not been investigated previously for this purpose. It is observed that the gerundial pattern has indeed become more frequent in relation to the *to* infinitive, but it is also shown in the chapter that *to* infinitives were very frequent in the nineteenth century, including cases where the lower clause is in the passive. By contrast, in current English such complements with *to* infinitives are quite rare. The chapter offers a grammar internal explanation for this finding, linking it to a change in the syntactic status of infinitival *to* in English, with corpus evidence documenting the change.

Keywords Great complement shift • Diachronic change • Corpus linguistics

© The Author(s) 2019
M. Kaunisto, J. Rudanko, *Variation in Non-finite Constructions in English*, https://doi.org/10.1007/978-3-030-19044-6_4

4.1   Introduction

Consider the sentences in (1a–b).

(1) a. She would not submit to be one of many, and besides she loved
   and she eloped with her beloved. (COHA, 1899, NF)
   b. They submitted to giving up twenty per cent of their profits on
   the pre-war standard: [...] (Hansard, House of Commons,
   May 18, 1916)

The sentences in (1a–b) show that the matrix verb *submit* has selected two
types of non-finite complements in recent English. In sentence (1a) the
complement is of course a *to* infinitive sentence, and in (1b) the sentential
complement may be termed a *to -ing* complement, where the complement
consists of the preposition *to* and a following gerund. While the verb *submit* is intransitive in both (1a–b), the verb *submit* can also be used in other
ways. For instance, it can be used transitively with nonsentential comple-
ments, as in ... *he had submitted plans for the renovation of a major restau-
rant in Queens* ... (COHA, 1972, NEWS), and with sentential
complements, as in ... *I will not tamely and silently submit myself to be
butchered in cold blood* ... (COHA, 1834, FIC), but for practical reasons
the present study concentrates on the intransitive types illustrated
in (1a–b).

In both (1a) and (1b) the matrix verb *submit* assigns a semantic role to
its subject, and the sentences share the property of being subject control
constructions, with the higher subject controlling the reference of the
understood lower subject, which may be represented with the symbol PRO.

As regards the category status of infinitival *to*, it is accepted here that in
current English it is under the Aux node. As Warner (1993, 64) notes, the
best piece of evidence is that infinitival *to* permits ellipsis of the type *He
wants to go to the cinema, but I don't want to.* (The example has been
modified from Radford 1997, 53.) The ellipsis has been called VP
Deletion, but Warner's term "post-auxiliary ellipsis" seems preferable, as
he argues (Warner 1993, 5–6). This parallels post-auxiliary ellipsis possibilities with conventional auxiliaries, as in *He cannot go to the cinema, but
I can.* By contrast, prepositional *to* does not permit the ellipsis of the constituent that follows, as in *He wants to go to the cinema, but I don't want
to go to.* (The example has again been modified from Radford 1997, 53.)

Using traditional labels for syntactic categories, the relevant parts of sentences (1a–b) can then be represented as in (1a′–b′) in their essential parts.

(1) a′. [[she]$_{NP}$ would not [[submit]$_{Verb}$ [[PRO]$_{NP}$ [to]$_{Aux}$ [be part of many]$_{VP}$]$_{S2}$]$_{VP}$]$_{S1}$

b′. [[they]$_{NP}$ [[submitted]$_{Verb}$ [[to]$_{Prep}$ [[[PRO]$_{NP}$ [[giving up]$_{Verb}$ [twenty per cent of their profits]$_{NP}$]$_{VP}$]$_{S2}$]$_{NP}$]$_{PP}$]$_{VP}$]$_{S1}$

The lower clause in (1b′) is bracketed as a sentence dominated by an NP, which captures the notion of a nominal clause, often used in the analysis of gerunds in traditional grammar.

The categorical distinctions made in (1a′–b′) suggest that the two types of complements are very different from a syntactic point of view. However, as was noted, the two types of constructions share the property of involving subject control. In addition, the two constructions are featured under the same sense of the matrix verb *submit* for instance in the *OED*. They are under sense I "to place oneself in a position of submission or compliance." Subsense 1 of sense I is defined as "to consent or condescend *to* do something," and intransitive uses with *to* infinitive and *to -ing* complements have been placed under that subsense in subsection 1.b, with the latter linked to "later use." It is reasonable to conclude from the *OED* treatment of the verb that the two constructions—"*submit to* Verb ..." and "*submit to* Verb*ing* ...," can be considered similar in meaning, and that their use merits investigation and comparison.

A first objective is to examine the incidence of the two types of constructions with *submit* in the course of the last two centuries and in very recent English, in both American and British English. The corpora with a diachronic orientation to be consulted are COHA and Hansard, and for very recent English the NOW Corpus is consulted, for both American and British English. It is noteworthy that some standard dictionaries, including the seventh edition of *the Oxford Advanced Learner's Dictionary of Current English* (Wehmeier et al. 2005) do not mention or illustrate either of the types of constructions in (1a–b), and it is therefore of interest to shed light on the recent use of the two variants. Section 4.2 of this chapter is devoted to this objective. A further objective is to investigate whether the use of the two types of complement with *submit* may be linked to the category status of infinitival *to*. This issue, picking up on a suggestion first brought up in Rudanko (2018, 99) in connection with a different higher predicate, is considered in Sect. 4.3.

4.2   To Infinitive and to -ing Complements of Submit in Recent English

To gain an overview of the recent history of *to* infinitival and *to -ing* complements of *submit* over the last centuries in American and British English, searches were made in COHA and in the Hansard Corpus. The text types of the two corpora do not match, but both are large and structured corpora, and they are suitable for comparing historical trends, given the corpora currently available. For practical reasons every third decade was chosen in each corpus, beginning with the 1820s, and ending with the 2000s. The search strings used were simply "[submit].[v*] to [v?i*]" for *to* infinitives and "[submit].[v*] to [v?g*]" for *to -ing* complements. Regarding recall, the search strings do not retrieve tokens with insertions, but insertions can be expected to be rare since the constructions involve complements, and because insertions are not likely to favour one of these types of complements over the other (see Tyrkkö and Rudanko forthcoming). As for precision, quite a large number of tokens are also retrieved that are not directly relevant, especially in the case of the search string for *to* infinitives. Illustrations of such tokens are given in (2a–e).

(2) a. […] it implements the promise in the Gracious Speech that legislation would be submitted to ensure that during the transition from war to peace there are available such powers […] (Hansard, House of Commons, Oct. 9, 1945)

   b. He submitted to capture in absolute silence. (COHA, 1916, FIC)

   c. […] for the last ten years the steel industry has submitted to open public supervision of its prices and price policy […] (Hansard, House of Commons, May 28, 1945)

   d. If we accept the position that we should not submit to force within our own territories, I find it very difficult to see how we can deny the same position to our Dutch Allies […] (Hansard, House of Commons, Dec. 11, 1945)

   e. A woman married to this kind of man will sacrifice, without thought of self, for the sake of her family and to maintain harmony at home: People wonder why she submits: She submits to maintain harmony in the home because she knows that disharmony is hurtful to the children […] (Hansard, House of Lords, June 12, 1975)

Tokens of the type of (2a) are very frequent in the material. In them the matrix verb *submit* is in the passive, with its subject corresponding to its logical object, but in their case the verb has a meaning different from that in (1a–b) and the constructions do not involve complements with subject control in the first instance. Tokens of type of (2b–d) are also very frequent, and while the verb *submit* in them has the meaning also found in (1a–b), the complement that follows the word *to* is a non-sentential NP, and neither a *to* infinitive nor a gerund. Heads of such NPs include *capture*, *supervision* and *force*, as found in (2b–d), and they often lack an article, but their nominal status can still be clear, as in (2b–d). The fact that they are found among the results of the search query as outlined above is due to the erroneous tagging of the word following *to* as a verb.

As for the type of the sentence illustrated in (2e), it is not frequent, but still possible. In it the sense of the verb *submit* is similar to that found in (1a–b) and in this case, what follows *submit* is a *to* infinitive clause. However, this sentence represents a usage where the following *to* infinitive is an adjunct, and not a complement. That is, the key part of the extract is interpreted to mean approximately 'she submits (to her husband/to her husband's unsavory conduct) in order to maintain harmony in the home,' with the *to* infinitive functioning as an adjunct of purpose.

There is still another type of search result of "[submit].[v*] to [v?*g]" in the data that deserves a comment at this point. Consider (3a–b):

(3) a. A wild cat, for instance, will not submit to caressing; it has no sense of gratitude. (COHA, 1919, MAG)
   b. But some students are now being forced to drink excessive amounts of alcohol and submit to paddling or beating. (COHA, 2002, MAG)

The question in sentences of the type of (3a–b) is whether the *-ing* construction should be analyzed as verbal—and therefore as a sentential complement with an understood subject—or as a nominal, that is, as a non-sentential NP. Huddleston and Pullum (2002, 1199–1200) do not discuss the precise type of construction illustrated in (3a–b), but they offer comments on sentences with non-prepositional gerunds such as *The children need coaxing*. They make the following key point:

In [i] [their sentence *The children need coaxing*, MK and JR] *coaxing* can be a verb, "to be coaxed," or a noun, as in *They need a little coaxing*, but we understand that the coaxing should apply to the children, so the meaning is effectively the same as with the verbal meaning. (Huddleston and Pullum 2002, 1200)

Huddleston and Pullum (2002, 1199–1200) use the term "concealed passive construction" to refer to the type of gerundial example illustrated. They discuss non-prepositional gerunds, but do not discuss the *to -ing* pattern in this connection. However, sentences (3a–b) appear to be similar to their sentence, since for instance in (3a) it is clear that the caressing, if it were to take place, would apply to the referent of the subject of the higher sentence, as in Huddleston and Pullum's sentence, and that the key part of the sentence might be rephrased as *A wild cat will not submit to being caressed*, with an explicit or overt passive. Of course, the *-ing* construction may be modified in a way that excludes a verbal interpretation and only permits a nominal interpretation, as for instance in *A wild cat will not submit to caressing of any kind*, where the addition *of any kind* has been taken from Huddleston and Pullum (2002, 1200). (Such an addition would clearly not be compatible with an explicit passive: *A wild cat will not submit to being caressed of any kind.*) However, for sentences such as (3a–b), which lack such modification and which do permit an explicit passive as a variant, the present authors adopt the idea that a verbal interpretation is possible, on the analogy of the example *The children need coaxing* from Huddleston and Pullum (2002, 1200), and that it is possible to use the term "concealed passive" for sentences of the type of (3a–b). In other words, it is suggested here that the term "concealed passive" can be extended to at least one type of prepositional gerund.

With the comments above taken for granted, the numerical results obtained from COHA and Hansard are presented in Table 4.1, with

Table 4.1 *To* infinitive and *to -ing* complements of *submit* in selected decades of COHA and the Hansard Corpus (numbers in parentheses indicate frequencies per million words)

Decade	American English (COHA)		British English (Hansard)	
	to *inf.*	to -ing	to *inf.*	to -ing
1820s	22 (3.2)	0	48 (4.1)	1 (0.1)
1850s	36 (2.2)	1 (0.1)	105 (3.2)	2 (0.1)
1880s	33 (1.6)	12 (0.6)	63 (1.1)	7 (0.1)
1910s	6 (0.3)	17 (0.7)	40 (0.5)	20 (0.3)
1940s	4 (0.2)	3 (0.1)	2 (0.0)	10 (0.1)
1970s	1 (0.0)	1 (0.0)	3 (0.0)	8 (0.0)
2000s	1 (0.0)	4 (0.1)	0	2 (0.0)

normalized frequencies (per million words) given in parentheses. Some illustrations are given in (4a–d), from COHA for American English, and in (5a–d), from Hansard, for British English.

(4) a. For my own part, I would as soon submit to talk the dialect of a Yorkshireman, or Lancasterman, or Bow-bell-man, in London. (COHA, 1823, FIC)
   b. I know; but what can you expect when superior people must submit to be judged by mobs? (COHA, 1948, MAG)
   c. I was brought up in the yard, remember, and to a certain extent I have to submit to being weighed in the yard's own scales. (COHA, 1882, FIC)
   d. Of course we had to show identification and submit to being frisked before they would let us enter the bulletproof area. (COHA, 2003, MAG)

(5) a. [...] he would never submit to have the constituted powers of the country dictated to by any individual whatever [...] (Hansard, House of Commons, Jan. 31, 1821)
   b. [...] the people of this country will not, over time, submit to be taxed otherwise than by the authority of this House, [...] (Hansard, House of Commons, Mar. 18, 1975)
   c. [...] the French Government had never submitted to having that subject called in question: [...] (Hansard, House of Commons, July 22, 1850)
   d. The hon. Gentleman said that he would not submit to sitting in an assembly to which he had been elected as a result of the added voted or preferences of supporters of other parties: [...] (Hansard, House of Commons, Jan. 12, 1978)

The information in Table 4.1 shows that *to* infinitives were much more frequent than *to -ing* complements with the matrix verb *submit* in the nineteenth century. In the first two decades investigated no tokens at all of the latter type were encountered in American English, and in British English the numbers were also very low. However, in the 1880s the gerundial pattern had become a noteworthy type of complement with *submit*, especially in American English, and by the 1910s the gerundial pattern had become more frequent than the *to* infinitive in American English, with the *to* infinitive going down in frequency in a dramatic fashion. In British English the *to* -*ing* pattern had also gone up in frequency in relation to the *to* infinitive, compared to the 1880s, but it still lagged behind the *to* infinitive by some way. By the 1940s the *to* -*ing* pattern had overtaken the *to* infinitive in British English, but the frequencies of both were in decline. The general decline has been continuing, except that in the 2000s there may again be the possibility of a rising trend in American English. Overall, the figures in Table 4.1 testify to a dramatic change in favour of the *to* -*ing* pattern, combined with a later sharp decline in the frequency of both patterns. The initial spread of the gerundial pattern in relation to the *to* infinitive is in accordance with a major aspect of the Complement Shift. The later decline of the *to* -*ing* construction in the historical corpora makes it all the more important to investigate the question in current English.

To gain further information on the situation in current English it is advisable to turn to the NOW Corpus, containing texts from newspapers and magazines on the web. It offers the advantage that both American English and British English can be compared with data from the same corpus. Both segments are very large, and the size of the American English part is 972.5 million words and that of the British English part is 786.9 million words. The two parts of the NOW Corpus were analyzed using the same principles as were applied in the case of COHA and Hansard above. Table 4.2 gives information on the frequencies of *to* infinitives and *to* -*ing* complements in the American English and British English segments of the NOW Corpus.

Examples from the American English part of the NOW Corpus are given in (6a–b) and from the British English part in (7a–b).

(6) a. Within the frame of the Gothic loop a previously repressed event of the past suddenly imposes itself upon the present and refuses to leave an attempt to haunt the minds of the protagonists until

Table 4.2 Frequencies of *to* infinitives and *to* -*ing* complements in the American and British English parts of the NOW Corpus, with normalized frequencies, per million words, in parentheses

Part of NOW	to infinitives	to -ing complements
American English	16 (0.02)	66 (0.07)
British English	7 (0.01)	28 (0.03)

they submit to face the challenge which the processing of that past memory has to offer. (NOW, US, 2014, *Student Pulse*)

b. She had to undergo an invasive rape exam, to submit to being intimately photographed by police [...] (NOW, US, 2018, *Arkansas Online*)

(7) a. Charles Dickens described in the Pickwick Papers how young women "screamed and struggled, and ran into corners, and did everything but leave the room, until... they all at once found it useless to resist any longer and submitted to be kissed with a good grace." (NOW, GB, 2015, *Telegraph.co.uk*)

b. Tesco's reaction was to remove the provenance and cravenly submit to discarding a point of difference between Scottish produce and other produce. (NOW, GB, 2016, *Herald Scotland*)

The figures in Table 4.2 show that both constructions are relatively rare, especially in British English, but they also show that both constructions do still occur and that the gerundial construction is clearly the more frequent one in both American and British English. It is hard to compare the figures in Table 4.2 to the figures for the 2000s in COHA, because the American English part of the NOW Corpus is so much larger than the segment for the 2000s in COHA, but the frequencies in Table 4.2 testify to the presence of the gerundial pattern in very recent American English. The infinitival pattern is considerably less frequent but is still found as well. In British English the gerundial pattern is much less frequent than the corresponding pattern in American English, and the infinitival pattern is approximately as rare as in American English, but both patterns still merit recognition.

What is striking about the NOW data is the large number of concealed passives, especially in the American English data. It bears reiterating that an *-ing* form preceded by *submit to* is not always a concealed passive. It is nominal when it occurs in an environment that shows it to be nominal, precluding an interpretation as a concealed passive. To illustrate, consider sentence (8), from the American English part of the NOW Corpus:

(8) Comcast wants to make sure devices our customers purchase at retail will work well and are safe, and we have not asked Zoom to submit to testing that is any different than what we ask of every other cable modem manufacturer we work with. (NOW, US, 2010, *Ars Technica*)

The relative clause that follows the *-ing* form *testing* in (8) shows that *testing* is nominal in this case, and not verbal and thus not a concealed passive.[1] (It can be noted that an overt passive, as in *＊we have not asked Zoom to submit to being tested that is any different than what we ask every other cable modem manufacturer...* is not a possible variant in this case.) However, there are numerous instances in the American English part of the NOW Corpus where an *-ing* form following the substring *submit to* can be interpreted as a concealed passive. Two examples are given in (9a–b).

(9) a. [...] the winning bidder must submit to testing for sexually transmitted infections prior to the encounter [...] (NOW, US, 2012, *The Atlantic*)

b. Last summer, Claywell was ordered to submit to questioning about his finances by federal prosecutors, [...] (NOW, US, 2018, *Hartford Courant*)

In sentence (9a), for instance, an overt passive is possible: ... *the winning bidder must submit to being tested for sexually transmitted infections prior to the encounter.* The same is true of sentence (9b). Examples of such concealed passives have been included in the totals in Table 4.2. The present study in fact suggests that they have become more frequent in very recent American English. The decades considered from COHA amount to approximately 144 million words, but in the whole of that material there are only three concealed passives selected by *submit*, amounting to a frequency of 0.02 per million. (One of the three is from 2002, thus representing recent usage.) On the other hand, in the American English part of the NOW Corpus, the present investigators have counted as many 33 of them, amounting to a frequency of 0.03 per million. As was noted above, the *-ing* forms in question may be ambiguous, especially when standing alone, between a verbal and a nominal interpretation. The verbal interpretation, when possible, represents a concealed passive and the close proximity of concealed passives to NPs may be offering a pathway for the increasing spread of concealed passives with *submit*, given that the verb in the relevant sense also frequently selects *to* NP complements, as illustrated in (2b–d) above. The suggestion made here about an increasing trend in the incidence of concealed passives is naturally subject to further investigation.

4.3 FURTHER DISCUSSION OF THE FINDINGS

In Chap. 3 the Choice Principle was seen to be a factor bearing on the complement selection properties of the adjective *frightened*, with *to* infinitives linked to [+Choice] environments and *of -ing* complements linked to [−Choice] environments. The question then arises as to whether it may play a role in the complement selection of the matrix verb *submit*. It should of course be borne in mind that the Choice Principle is only applicable when there is considerable variation between an infinitival and gerundial pattern. The American English part of the NOW Corpus suggests itself for investigation here, with **16** *to* infinitives and **66** gerundial complements. Table 4.3 offers information on *to* infinitive and *to -ing* complements of *submit* in [+Choice] and [−Choice] contexts in that part of the NOW Corpus. The Chi Square is 10.67, and the results are significant (df = 1, $p < 0.01$).

Illustrations of [+Choice] environments are given in (10a–b), and of [−Choice] contexts in (11a–b), all from the American English part of the NOW Corpus.

(10) a. A Muslim is one who submits to do the fill of Allah (God) ... (NOW, US, 2010, *Hip-Hop Wired*)
    b. He knows he has no skills, he knows he has to submit to starting at the ground level and working his way into a sport in which he is a latecomer. (NOW, US, 2016, *The Register-Guard*)
(11) a. As he has in the past, Giuliani would not say specifically whether Trump would submit to be questioned. (NOW, US, 2018, *Virginian-Pilot*)
    b. Prison staffers decided Padilla needed to be taken out of his cell and forced to take emergency medication, but he refused to voluntarily submit to being handcuffed and removed. (NOW, US, 2014, *The Sacramento Bee*)

Table 4.3 [+Choice] and [−Choice] complements of the verb *submit* in the American English part of the NOW Corpus

	[+Choice]	*[−Choice]*	*Total*
to infinitives	12	4	16
to -ing	18	48	66

As for the historical corpora, decades of considerable variation between the two non-finite patterns are not easy to find, and the Choice Principle seems less applicable. However, there is one aspect of the historical data that merits closer discussion here. Concentrating on the Hansard Corpus, the most suitable starting point might be the 1910s in Hansard where there are 4 *to* infinitives and 20 *to -ing* complements of *submit*, as noted in Table 4.1. Of the 40 *to* infinitives, 15 are [+Choice] and 25 are [−Choice], and of the 20 *to -ing* complements, 4 are [+Choice] and 16 are [−Choice]. The proportion of [+Choice] environments in the case of *to* infinitives is thus some 37.5 per cent, while it is only a quarter in the case of *to -ing* complements. This is consistent with the Choice Principle. However, these numbers do not reach statistical significance, and what is noteworthy and of theoretical interest is that a high number, more than half, of the 40 *to* infinitival complements occur in [−Choice] environments. The figures for the 1910s are not a one-time aberration. In the 1850s the number of *to* infinitives is 105, as shown in Table 4.1, and of these, a clear majority are again found with [−Choice] lower predicates. The same is true of the figures for the 1880s, where the total of *to* infinitives is 63, and of these as many as 49 are in [−Choice] environments. On the other hand, in the 1940s the total number of [−Choice] environments of *to* infinitival complements of *submit* (together with the total number of *to* infinitives) is down to only 2.

The change relating to the incidence of [−Choice] contexts described above merits further discussion. As a first step it is appropriate to begin with a comment on the nature of [−Choice] environments of *to* infinitive complements of *submit* in the 1850s, 1880s, and 1910s. Consider the sentences in (12a–c), all from the Hansard Corpus.

(12) a. Another reason was, that a system of national education required an outlay of public money, the Dissenters would not submit to be taxed even for secular purposes [...] (Hansard, House of Commons, June 5, 1850)

b. [...] at last he had to submit to be carried, bag and baggage, to the Metropolis from the country [...] (Hansard, House of Commons, May 12, 1881)

c. Although we have passed through centuries of oppression and ascendancy, we will never sit down and submit to be hated and despised in our own country. (Hansard, House of Commons, June 9, 1913)

In sentences (12a–c) the lower sentence is in the passive and the understood subject NP of the lower sentence represents the logical object of the verb of the lower sentence. Therefore it typically has the role of Patient or Undergoer, which is the semantic role that is the furthest removed from the Agent role. The environment is therefore prototypically [–Choice] (see for instance Rudanko 2012).

There is little doubt that the decline of *to* infinitives of *submit* in [–Choice] environments—and in [+Choice] environments—should be understood against the general background of the Great Complement Shift, since a major aspect of the shift concerns the spread of -*ing* complements at the expense of *to* infinitives, and initially, in the 1880s and 1910s, *to* -*ing* complements do become more prominent with *submit* in relation to *to* infinitives. At the same time, it may be helpful in this connection to refer to another major change in the history of English that relates to *to* infinitives specifically, even if it only provides context for the Great Complement Shift, without being part of it as such.

In Sect. 4.1 it was pointed out that in current English infinitival *to* should be analyzed as an auxiliary, and that the best piece of evidence for this analysis has to do with post-auxiliary ellipsis, as in *He wants to go to the cinema but I don't want to*, which parallels ellipsis with conventional auxiliaries, as in *He cannot go to the cinema, but I can*. However, it should be pointed that the status of infinitival *to* and the nature of the *to* infinitive have themselves undergone change in the history of English. In Old English the *to* infinitive was "essentially nominal [...] but with already some verbal features incorporated" (Fischer 1996, 131; see also Los 2015, 144–145, who pays attention to verbal features of the *to* infinitive even in Old English). The later overall evolution of the *to* infinitive has been summed up concisely by Denison, who points to the "drift of the English infinitive from a nominal to a verbal character, now virtually complete, and the concomitant dissociation of the infinitive marker *to* from the homonymous preposition" (Denison 1998, 266). The verbal character of infinitival *to* in current English is reflected in it being categorized as an auxiliary. However, as Denison also points out, the post-auxiliary ellipsis construction with *to*—the best piece of evidence for the auxiliary status of infinitival *to*—only began to gain in frequency from the middle of the nineteenth century onwards. As Denison puts it, "until the mid-nineteenth century and after, most writers avoided it" [the post-auxiliary ellipsis construction involving *to*], but "from then on [...] what had been a trickle of examples soon turned into a flood" (Denison 1998, 201).

Denison does not provide numerical evidence of how a "trickle" turned into a "flood." Because the issue is pertinent to the analysis of *to* infinitives, the present authors chose some common verbs from among the ordinary subject control verbs listed in Rudanko (1989, 22–23) in order to see how well Denison's point holds up with them. The verbs selected were *like, mean, try, want*, and *wish*, and post-auxiliary ellipsis possibilities were investigated with their help in the period from the 1820s to the 1870s in COHA and in Hansard. Such an investigation cannot exhaust the subject, but it can still shed light on the issue, since the verbs were not chosen with any kind of predetermined outcome in mind. The search strings consisted of a verb (each of the five) followed by *to* and a comma or a period. Two illustrations of post-auxiliary ellipsis are given in (13a–b).

(13) a. I say let every man bake his bread in the gov'ment oven, if he likes to. (COHA, 1842, FIC)
b. The noble Lord says he does not want to gag the house: Though he may not want to, he is taking a very good chance of doing it: [...] (Hansard, House of Commons, May 3, 1861)

In addition, the search string used also brought to light four tokens, all in Hansard, of what has been called shared string coordination constructions (Radford 1997, 105–107), as in (14). These may be included here because the shared string coordination construction has also been taken to be a test of constituency (Radford 1997, 106), and what is shared in this case is a VP, separated from *to*.

(14) He would not, nor did he wish to, attribute that motive to the hon. and learned Gentleman [...] (Hansard, House of Commons, Mar. 6, 1835)

Information on the incidence of the post-auxiliary ellipsis and shared string coordination constructions in the decades from the 1820s to the 1870s is given in Table 4.4.

The analyst needs to approach the low numbers in the Hansard column with caution, because of the difference in text type and because of potential transcription issues. Post-auxiliary ellipsis may well have had a colloquial or informal flavour, which is illustrated in example (13a), and members of the Commons and the Lords might have preferred to avoid that kind of flavour in Parliamentary debates. Or transcribers might well

Table 4.4 Post-auxiliary ellipsis and shared string coordination with selected verbs from the 1820s to the 1870s

Decade	COHA (pmw)	Hansard (pmw)
1820s	7 (1.01)	0
1830s	13 (0.94)	1 (0.04)
1840s	40 (2.49)	2 (0.07)
1850s	76 (4.61)	0
1860s	173 (10.10)	2 (0.06)
1870s	215 (11.55)	6 (0.16)

have preferred to avoid informality when transcribing debates, and preparing them for publication, in favour of a more formal style (see Slembrouck 1992; Mollin 2007).

In order to further investigate occurrence of post-auxiliary ellipsis with the selected verbs in another corpus of historical British English texts, the Corpus of Late Modern English Texts 3.0 (henceforth CLMET3.0; see Diller et al. 2011) was examined. Although the corpus is smaller in size, it does contain texts representing different genres. The corpus consists of three diachronic subsections, namely sections representing the periods 1710–1780, 1780–1850, and 1850–1920. Focusing on the last two subsections, which contain 11.6 and 12.6 million words, respectively, searches were made with the AntConc concordancer (see e.g. Anthony 2013) for the five verbs followed by either a comma or a period. Two illustrations of relevant tokens are given in (15a–b), the first from the 1780–1850 section of the corpus, and (15b) from the 1850–1920 section.

(15) a. 'You never heard anything more of that rascal, I suppose, eh?' 'Not a syllable,' replied Hugh. 'I never want to. I don't believe I ever shall. He's dead long ago, I hope.' (CLMET3.0, Part 2 (1780–1850), Charles Dickens, *Barnaby Rudge* (1839))
b. "Crouch lower!" said Julien. "If any one wanted to, they could count your eyelashes from the windows." (CLMET3.0, Part 3 (1850–1920), Enid Algerine Bagnold, *The Happy Foreigner* (1920))

In the 1780–1850 section, tokens of post-auxiliary ellipsis were few in number, with only three relevant tokens found. In contrast, the pattern is notably more common in the third subsection of the corpus, with altogether 103 occurrences of the selected verbs with post-auxiliary ellipsis. Because of the structure of the corpus, the CLMET3.0 data does not lend itself easily to a decade-by-decade analysis, but it is noteworthy that all of the tokens in the 1850–1920 section of the corpus were found in texts published after 1870, and as many as 85 out of the 103 tokens appeared in texts published post-1890.

Together with the findings in the CLMET3.0 data, the numbers in American English in Table 4.4 show that Denison was quite right in talking about a "trickle" turning into a "flood": there was indeed a spectacular increase in the use of the post-auxiliary ellipsis at least in American English from the middle of the nineteenth century onwards in the text types covered in COHA. The findings altogether also suggest that the increasing use of post-auxiliary ellipsis may have taken place earlier in American English than in British English.

What the spectacular increase in the use of the post-auxiliary ellipsis construction means is that after the mid-nineteenth century onwards, infinitival *to* gradually acquired its present status under the auxiliary node. The question is then as to what its grammatical status was prior to that time. The present authors would not presume to give a final answer to this question here, but they suggest that the grammatical boundary between infinitival *to* and prepositional *to* may have been felt by speakers to be more fuzzy before the middle of the nineteenth century. It is possible that the *to* infinitive was felt to be more nominal before infinitival *to* came to be used in the post-auxiliary ellipsis construction. This suggestion would then at least partly explain the ease with which *submit* selected infinitival complements of the [–Choice] type in the nineteenth century. When the auxiliary status of infinitival *to* began to be gradually solidified from the middle of the nineteenth century onwards, infinitival *to* also diverged from prepositional *to* more definitely, allowing the *to -ing* construction increasingly to move into the more nominal space formerly occupied by the *to* infinitive and to have a more clearly defined role linked to [–Choice] contexts. This would have been a natural development given that gerundial complements are at the nominal end of the scale of nouniness of sentential complements (cf. Ross 2004) and given that *submit* has frequently selected *to* NP complements during the period investigated here (see Note 1). Further, if post-auxiliary ellipsis occurred earlier in American English and only later in British English, as suggested by the numbers of tokens in COHA, the Hansard Corpus, and CLMET3.0, it would also follow that the rise of the *to -ing* pattern occurred slightly earlier in American English than in British English.

4.4 Concluding Remarks

The verb *submit* selects two non-finite involving subject control complements—*to* infinitives and *to -ing* complements—and this chapter follows their evolution in the course of the last two centuries. Attention is paid to both American and British English, with data from COHA, for American English, from the Hansard Corpus for British English, and from the NOW Corpus for very recent usage in both. It is observed that the *to* infinitive was clearly predominant in both regional varieties in the 1820s and 1850s, but in the 1880s noticeable numbers of *to -ing* complements were also encountered, especially in American English. In American English the *to -ing* pattern surpassed the *to* infinitive in the 1910s, with the numbers of *to* infinitives going down dramatically in that regional variety. In British English the number of *to* infinitives had also gone down dramatically by the 1940s, with *to -ing* complements surpassing them in frequency in that decade. For its part, the NOW Corpus shows that in very recent English there are noticeable numbers of *to -ing* complements selected by the verb in American English, but in British English their frequency is lower, and the numbers of *to* infinitives are relatively low in both.

The chapter also showed that in very recent American English, as represented in the NOW Corpus, the Choice Principle is a factor with an impact on complement selection. It was suggested that what have been termed concealed passives are relatively frequent in the NOW Corpus, and their [−Choice] character bears on the relevance of the Choice Principle. As for the evolution of the complement selection properties of the verb *submit*, attention was drawn to the presence of large numbers of *to* infinitives in [−Choice] contexts in several of the early decades of the Hansard Corpus investigated, and to the sharp drop in their numbers in the early twentieth century. The Great Complement Shift makes it possible to understand these findings, but the present authors also made the more specific suggestion that the change may be linked to a change in the grammatical status of infinitival *to*, and with the drift of *to* infinitives from a nominal to a verbal character, pointed out by Denison (1998). The authors investigated corpus data to shed light on the incidence of the post-auxiliary ellipsis construction, which has a crucial bearing on the analysis of infinitival *to*, and suggested that the more nominal space vacated by infinitival *to* may be a factor promoting the spread of the *to -ing* pattern, especially in [−Choice] contexts. It is a fascinating area within the system of English predicate complementation and will be worth watching in years to come.

NOTE

1. While it is appropriate to restrict the term "concealed passive" to verbal constructions, it can be noted that even though *testing* in (8) in the text is a noun, it still has a passive like interpretation. This is also the case with many NPs whose heads do not have the morphology of an *-ing* form. For instance, *He submitted to a test* means that he was tested. NPs with such nouns as their heads are very frequent with *submit to*. Thus all the NPs in (2b–d) in Section 1 are of this type. Other recent examples include (ia–c), which are from COHA, and (iia–c), which are from Hansard.

> (i) a. To gain that privilege, passengers must submit to an extensive background check, [...] (COHA, 2004, MAG)
> b. They do not want to submit to ritual circumcision. (COHA, 2004, NEWS)
> c. ... we should never order or submit to a high-tech medical test without weighing both the benefits and the risks. (COHA, 2004, MAG)
> (ii) a. I would take his words more seriously if he did not submit to what I call the Opposition's "year zero" approach [...] (Hansard, House of Commons, Apr. 11, 2002)
> b. Those countries have not freed themselves from the yoke of Soviet centralisation to submit to the same from Brussels. (Hansard, House of Commons, Dec. 2, 2002)
> c. I urge my hon. Friend not to stop debating the bill and not to submit to the pressure [...] (Hansard, House of Commons, May 10, 2002)

Examples of the same type are also abundant in earlier decades, and because the meaning of *submit* in them is similar to its meaning with *to* infinitive and *to -ing* complements, it is worth giving some of these here. The examples in (iiia–c) and (va–c) are from COHA and those in (iva–c) and (via–c) from Hansard. For reasons of space, illustrations are limited to tokens from the middle and the beginning of the period under review.

> (iii) a. But let me tell you that you are making a big mistake and it will cost you dear if you make me submit to this indignity. (COHA, 1911, FIC)
> b. "If we stay here and submit to capture," Ned replied, "it is all off for all of us. [...]" (COHA, 1911, FIC)
> c. [...] he was obliged to submit to considerable banter and to suffer some hard knocks from those present. (COHA, 1911, MAG)

(iv) a. We have had to submit to too much of this contemptuous treatment by the House of Lords in this House [...] (Hansard, House of Commons, Mar. 1, 1910)

b. Discussions of this nature will be a sheer waste of time, inasmuch as it may be taken as an absolute and settled fact that the people of this country will not submit to any tax whatever on foodstuffs imported into this country [...] (Hansard, House of Commons, Feb. 23, 1910)

c. [...] taxpayers have been willing to go on paying their taxes and to submit to the demands of the Excise officers [...] (Hansard, House of Commons, Mar. 21, 1910)

(v) a. Rouse your spirit, for heaven's sake; do not submit to such tyranny. (COHA, 1822, FIC)

b. No gentleman, no man of honourable feeling—no man of proper sensibility—would submit to the interference of a stranger. (COHA, 1822, FIC)

c. Would you then submit to oppression? (COHA, 1822, MAG)

(vi) a. And as she was a person who had the sense and spirit not to submit to wanton injuries, the event did take place. (Hansard, House of Commons, Feb. 6, 1821)

b. [...] they would not submit to the worst form of despotic oppression [...] (Hansard, House of Commons, Feb. 21, 1821)

c. [...] we might at this moment have been obliged to submit to arbitrary imprisonment, to torture [...] (Hansard, House of Commons, Feb. 21, 1821)

The ease with which illustrations can be found from within one year is a sign that the verb *submit*, with a meaning that is similar to its meaning with *to* infinitive and *to -ing* complements, has freely selected non-sentential *to* NP complements during the past two centuries.

REFERENCES

Anthony, Laurence. 2013. Developing AntConc for a New Generation of Corpus Linguists. In *Proceedings of the Corpus Linguistics Conference* (CL 2013), July 22–26, 2013, ed. A. Hardie and R. Love, 14–16. Lancaster: University Centre for Computer Corpus Research on Language.

Denison, David. 1998. Syntax. In *Cambridge History of the English Language*, ed. Susanne Romaine, vol. 4, 92–329. Cambridge: Cambridge University Press.

Diller, Hans-Jürgen, Hendrik De Smet, and Jukka Tyrkkö. 2011. A European Database of Descriptors of English Electronic Texts. *The European English Messenger* 19: 21–35.

Fischer, Olga. 1996. The Status of *to* in Old English *To*-Infinitives. *Lingua* 99: 107–133.

Huddleston, Rodney, and Geoffrey K. Pullum. 2002. *The Cambridge Grammar of the English Language*. Cambridge: Cambridge University Press.

Los, Bettelou. 2015. *The Rise of the To-infinitive*. Oxford: Oxford University Press.

Mollin, Sandra. 2007. The Hansard Hazard: Gauging the Accuracy of British Parliamentary Transcripts. *Corpora* 2 (2): 187–210.

Radford, Andrew. 1997. *Syntactic Theory and the Structure of English. A Minimalist Approach*. Cambridge: Cambridge University Press.

Ross, John R. 2004. Nouniness. In *Fuzzy Grammar*, ed. B. Aarts, D. Denison, E. Keizer, and G. Popova, 351–422. Oxford: Oxford University Press.

Rudanko, Juhani. 1989. *Complementation and Case Grammar: A Syntactic and Semantic Study of Selected Patterns of Complementation in Present-Day English*. Albany, NY: SUNY Press.

———. 2012. Exploring Aspects of the Great Complement Shift, with Evidence from the *TIME* Corpus and COCA. In *The Oxford Handbook of the History of English*, ed. Terttu Nevalainen and Elizabeth Traugott, 222–232. Oxford: Oxford University Press.

———. 2018. Semantic Roles as a Factor Affecting Complement Choice: A Case Study with Data from COHA. In *Subordination in English: Synchronic and Diachronic Perspectives*, ed. Elena Seoane, Carlos Acuña-Fariña, and Ignacio Palacios-Martínez, 85–102. Berlin: De Gruyter Mouton.

Slembrouck, Stef. 1992. The Parliamentary Hansard 'Verbatim' Report: The Written Construction of Spoken Discourse. *Language and Literature* 1 (2): 101–119.

Tyrkkö, Jukka, and Juhani Rudanko. forthcoming. Grammar, Text Type, and Diachrony as Factors Influencing Complement Choice. In *Early American Englishes*, ed. Merja Kytö and Lucia Siebers. Amsterdam: John Benjamins.

Warner, Anthony R. 1993. *English Auxiliaries: Structure and History*. Cambridge Studies in Linguistics 66. Cambridge: Cambridge University Press.

Wehmeier, Sally, Colin McIntosh, and Joanna Turnbull, eds. 2005. *The Oxford Advanced Learner's Dictionary of English*. 7th ed. Oxford: Oxford University Press.

CHAPTER 5

Exceptions to Bach's Generalization in Inner and Outer Core Varieties of English: The Case of *Warn Against -ing*

Abstract This chapter contributes to the study of prepositional gerunds selected by verbs such as *warn*. Verbs of this type are special in that with gerundial complements, the omission of noun phrase objects have become more frequent than "regular" constructions with expressed objects, which observe Bach's Generalization. In the present study both overt and covert constructions selected by *warn* are investigated in five subsections of the GloWbE corpus. The purpose is to find out whether violations of Bach's Generalization are as widespread in other regional varieties as they are in recent American English and whether generalizations can be established among different regional varieties of English, relating to the inner and outer core. The results here shed light on an aspect of the Great Complement Shift in different regional varieties. A second major objective is to inquire into the nature of understood objects in the covert construction in different regional varieties, with special attention here given to Indian, Pakistani, and Philippine English. A central issue is whether understood objects in violations of Bach's Generalization should be assigned general or specific interpretations, and whether regional differences exist with respect to the interpretation of such understood objects.

Keywords Complementation • Corpus linguistics • Understood objects • Regional variation

© The Author(s) 2019
M. Kaunisto, J. Rudanko, *Variation in Non-finite Constructions in English*, https://doi.org/10.1007/978-3-030-19044-6_5

5.1   Introduction

One aspect of syntactic change and variation concerns variation in the complement selection properties of verbs, and this chapter examines NP objects of the verb *warn* in a particular configuration that displays interesting variation in this respect. To introduce the configuration in question and to explain its significance, consider first the sentences in (1a–b) and (2a–b), from Bach (1980, 304):

(1) a. Mary persuaded John to go.
   b. Mary promised John to go.

(2´) a. *I persuaded to go.
   b. I promised to go.

According to Bach, both (1a–b) are well formed.[1] At the same time, there is a robust difference in well-formedness between the sentences in (2a–b), for (2b) is well formed and (2a) is ill formed. The types of matrix verbs represented by *persuade* and *promise* can therefore be expected to differ in their grammar in a major way. Setting aside the details of Bach's own analytic approach to the difference between the classes of *persuade* and *promise*, it is helpful to begin by noting that both *persuade* and *promise* are matrix verbs that select sentential complements. In this analysis both the higher verbs and the lower verbs in (1a–b) have their own subjects and the NP *John* in both (1a) and (1b) is assigned a theta role by the higher verb. In (1a) *persuade* assigns the role of Patient or Undergoer to the NP *John*, and in (1b) the NP *John* expresses the addressee and may be labeled Goal. Since the NP *John* belongs to the higher sentence in both of (1a–b), it follows that the subjects of the lower verbs are implicit or understood. Not every linguist shares the idea of an understood subject, but the idea was present in traditional grammar for instance in the work of Jespersen ([1940] 1961, 140), and in current work the understood subjects in the structural representations of (1´a–b) are represented by the symbol PRO (see Chomsky 1981, 6 and Chomsky 1986, 142–156):

(1´) a. [[Mary]$_{NP}$ [persuaded]$_{Verb}$ [John]$_{NP}$ [[PRO]$_{NP}$ [to]$_{Aux}$ [go]$_{VP}$] $_{S2}$]$_{S1}$.
   b. [[Mary]$_{NP}$ [promised]$_{Verb}$ [John]$_{NP}$ [[PRO]$_{NP}$ [to]$_{Aux}$ [go]$_{VP}$]$_{S2}$]$_{S1}$.

The interpretation of PRO is different in the two sentences: in (1a) PRO is controlled by the higher object, and in (1b) PRO controlled by the higher subject. In other words, (1a) represents a case of object control, and (1b) represents subject control.

To explain the contrasting behavior of *persuade* and *promise* in sentences of the type of (2a) and (2b), Bach (1980, 304) suggested that verbs of the *persuade* type require the post-verbal NP to be present. To phrase this in terms of object control and subject control verbs, it is possible to say that the object of an object control verb in an object control construction cannot be deleted. This is the essence of what has come to be called Bach's Generalization. Rizzi (1986) has provided a clear formulation of the Generalization:

> In object control structures the object NP must be structurally represented. (Rizzi 1986, 503)

Bach's Generalization explains the contrast between the patterns illustrated in (1a–b) and (2a–b). At the same time, note should be taken of some fairly recent work that has questioned the status of Bach's Generalization. Landau (2013) merits some comment in this connection. He considers the verbs *convince, persuade,* and *urge,* noting that while *John convinced/persuaded Mary to leave* is well formed, **John convinced/persuaded to leave* is not. However, he suggests that the non-omissibility of the direct object "could be a lexical property of the verbs *convince, persuade,* and *urge*" (Landau 2013, 178). He points out that the "same verbs also require a direct object in non-control constructions, as in *John convinced/persuaded Mary of a certain conclusion,* which is good, while **John convinced/persuaded of a certain conclusion* is ill formed" (Landau 2013, 179). (Analogous sentences can be devised for *urge.*) An appeal to lexical rules is not an impossible solution, but the present authors still believe that Bach's Generalization is useful in the study of object control. As pointed out by Rickman and Rudanko (2018, 93), there are verbs, including *teach* and *instruct,* that select object control, as in *my father taught me to play baseball* (COCA, 2009, FIC), but do not select non-sentential Goal arguments, of the type **My father taught me to baseball.* Even with these verbs the direct object in the object control construction is hardly likely to be omitted, as in **My father taught to play baseball,* and the non-omissibility of the matrix object is such sentences is predicted by Bach's Generalization. Bach's Generalization is also helpful from a broader perspective (Rickman and Rudanko 2018, 94), for it stimulates further work on the incidence and the nature of implicit objects preceding sentential complements in different languages and in different historical periods of a particular language. Overall, then, the present authors regard Bach's Generalization as valuable in inviting work on the properties of different types of object control constructions.

Bach's Generalization is of course neither an absolute rule nor a linguistic universal. As was pointed out by Rizzi (1986), Italian, for instance tends to be more permissive in allowing zero controllers in object control constructions, where the controller of PRO in an object control structure is zero, rather than being structurally represented. Such constructions may be termed cases of covert object control. Covert object control constructions may also be viewed as involving a type of detransitivization.[2]

As far as English is concerned, the contrast between the patterns of *promise* and *persuade*, as observed in (1a) and (2a), is certainly a robust difference. However, even in English there are some exceptions to Bach's Generalization. Large electronic corpora, especially those compiled recently by Mark Davies at the Brigham Young University, offer an important new resource for their investigation, and they make it possible to shed light on this area of English grammar in a way that was hardly possible earlier. Rudanko and Rickman (2014) was a recent step in this direction. That study concerned sentential complements of the verb *warn* and noted the well-formedness of covert object control complements of the verb introduced by the preposition *against*. The verb clearly selects overt object control constructions, as in (3a–b), gleaned from the Corpus of Historical American English (COHA):

(3) a. I would warn her against paying exorbitant prices for books and objects of art. (COHA, 1922, FIC; cited in Rudanko and Rickman 2014, 213))
   b. Bingley must be warned against showing any particular attention in that direction. (COHA, 2006, FIC)

As illustrated by sentence (3b), tokens of the overt control type are sometimes passive in form.

However, the verb *warn* also permits covert object control constructions without any ill-formedness, as noted in Rudanko and Rickman (2014). Examples (4a–b) are given as illustrations:

(4) a. Telephoto surveillance cameras peer down, armed police patrol the border, bright yellow sign warn against taking any photo-

graphs or making so much as a note or a simple sketch, under penalties on the Internal Security Act. (COHA, 2001, NF)
b. In the speech, focused on Iraq, Mr. McCain will warn against making policy about the war based on "the temporary favor of the latest public opinion poll" [...] (COHA, 2007, NEWS)

Rudanko (2015, Chap. 8) was another study that brought corpus evidence to bear on the investigation of Bach's Generalization and of exceptions to it, and it concerned the verb *counsel*. This verb can be used as an object control verb, as in ... *I would never counsel you against being here ...* (COCA, 1996, SPOK), but it also permits covert objects control, contrary to Bach's Generalization, as in ... *the authors counsel against abruptly empowering people, ...* (COCA, 2005, ACAD).

Rudanko and Rickman (2014) and Rudanko (2015, Chap. 8) were based on data from American English only. The present study has the purpose of shedding further light on exceptions to Bach's Generalization in *against -ing* complements of the verb *warn* and their background. Another objective is to broaden the range to data first of all to British English, as the other major core variety of English, and then also to current usage from three regional varieties of an outer circle type. These are Indian English, Pakistani English, and Philippine English. Such outer circle varieties have so far not been investigated with respect to Bach's Generalization, and it is appropriate to begin to remedy this neglect. Naturally, it would be of interest to conduct studies of other regional varieties, and the limitation to the five considered here is because of practical reasons. As regards the choice of Indian, Pakistani, and Philippine English, it can be added that Indian and Pakistani English were selected because India and Pakistan have been and are part of the British Commonwealth and because of historical links between Great Britain and the two countries. However, because of sociocultural differences between these countries, it is interesting to examine whether the usage as regards the focus of the present study shows differences between these varieties of English. Some evidence has been found in earlier studies (see e.g. Shastri 1996) on the differences between the two varieties in the selection of sentential complements of verbs, nouns, and adjectives. As for Philippine English, the Philippines has had, and continues to have, close historical and administrative ties to the United States. A number of comparisons are offered regarding the frequency of violations of Bach's Generalization in the five regional varieties. Taking into account the historical links between Great

Britain and India and Pakistan, on the one hand, and those between the United States and the Philippines, on the other, the comparisons include comparing British English with Indian and Pakistani English and American English with Philippine English. From a qualitative perspective, comments are also provided on the nature of the covert objects in the different regional varieties considered.

5.2   The Diachronic Changes in the Occurrence of Overt and Covert Object Control Complements of *Warn*

Perhaps the most striking finding in Rudanko and Rickman (2014) regarding the incidence and nature of the covert object control pattern with *warn* was that the appearance of the covert pattern is a recent phenomenon in the history of English. This conclusion is based on the evidence of COHA. In the study COHA was surveyed decade by decade for tokens of *warn* (NP) + *against* + V_{ing}, and it was observed that while the overt object control pattern was found with a frequency of slightly below or at 1 per million words from the 1840s to the 1900s, the covert pattern was virtually nonexistent in the nineteenth century. In the decades from the 1910s to the 1980s the frequency of the overt pattern with *warn* fluctuated within a range of 0.8 to 1.1 per million words, and it declined to only about half of that in the 1990s and 2000s. As for the covert pattern, some tokens numbers began to be found in the first decades of the twentieth century, and in the period from the 1950s to the 1980s its frequency increased to a noticeable level, fluctuating between 0.5 and 0.7 per million words. In the last two full decades of COHA, the frequency of the covert pattern was 0.6 and 0.7 per million words, and in fact surpassed the frequency of the overt pattern. This is a remarkable turnaround, given the almost total absence of the covert object control construction in the data from COHA in the nineteenth century.

The rise of the covert object control pattern reported in the paragraph above suggests a recent change or a change in progress in English, with the intransitive pattern establishing itself as a new pattern of complementation, alongside of the transitive pattern, which is still retained of course. Since the findings reported in the previous paragraph were based solely on American English, it is natural to supplement the picture with data from British English. The Hansard Corpus, available online and containing speeches given in the British Parliament in 1803–2005, affords an opportunity to do so. It should of course be recognized that the text type of the Hansard Corpus is different from the text types of COHA, but from the point of view of investigating the system of the English predicate complementation, it can still be used as a source of data of authentic usage. For practical reasons this study deals with *warn*, as did Rudanko and Rickman (2014), and it is easy enough to investigate its complementation in the new corpus.

The search string used was "against [v*g?]" with "[warn].[v*]" within nine words to the left. The search string yields 1107 tokens in all.[3] Four duplicates or otherwise irrelevant tokens were excluded from the analysis. Two illustrations of the overt control pattern are given in (5a–b), and two illustrations of the covert pattern are given in (6a–b).

(5) a. ... I warn the Government against splitting up our forces into penny packets as token forces to be sent here, there and everywhere: ... (Hansard, House of Commons, Sept. 15, 1950)

   b. The noble Lord, Lord Rochester, warned me against making that statement ... (Hansard, House of Lords, July 15, 1991)

(6) a. In "The Times" today Lord Brand's letter warns strongly against taking the present situation in our terms of trade as likely to be permanent; ... (Hansard, House of Commons, June 3, 1954)

   b. ... while giving his blessing to rapid reform Mr. Gorbachev has also warned against forcing developments there: ... (Hansard, House of Lords, Jan. 17, 1990)

The findings on both the overt and the covert control patterns dependent on *warn* in the Hansard Corpus are given in Table 5.1. They are given decade by decade, with normalized frequencies, per million words, given in parentheses.

Taking the difference in text types into account, caution should be exercised when comparing the information in Table 5.1 with the corresponding data in the decades of COHA. However, the overall picture that emerges from the figures in Table 5.1 bears some remarkable similarities with the trends identified for American English on the basis of COHA. One important similarity is that the overt pattern was the dominant pattern throughout the nineteenth century by a very long way. Indeed, in the British English data the predominance of the overt pattern in that century

Table 5.1   The incidence overt and covert object control constructions with *warn* in the Hansard Corpus (pmw = frequency per million words)

Decade	Size	Overt tokens (pmw)	Covert tokens (pmw)
1800s	5.0	8 (1.6)	0
1810s	7.1	9 (1.3)	0
1820s	11.6	17 (1.5)	0
1830s	28.1	52 (1.9)	0
1840s	30.4	71 (2.3)	0
1850s	33.0	77 (2.3)	0
1860s	34.2	73 (2.1)	1 (0.0)
1870s	37.1	77 (2.1)	0
1880s	60.0	88 (1.5)	0
1890s	51.2	59 (1.2)	1 (0.0)
1900s	64.7	57 (0.9)	0
1910s	79.8	51 (0.6)	0
1920s	71.7	40 (0.6)	0
1930s	95.2	45 (0.5)	1 (0.0)
1940s	94.8	38 (0.4)	1 (0.0)
1950s	121.0	47 (0.4)	2 (0.0)
1960s	152.0	52 (0.3)	8 (0.1)
1970s	163.3	47 (0.3)	5 (0.0)
1980s	183.7	54 (0.3)	22 (0.1)
1990s	177.1	52 (0.3)	21 (0.1)
2000s	88.4	15 (0.2)	12 (0.1)

is even more pronounced than in American English data, with this conclusion resting on the normalized frequencies of the two patterns. Another similarity is that it is only in very recent English that the covert pattern has begun to become more noticeable. At the same time, the comparison also suggests that the increasing use of the covert pattern began earlier in American English. The changes in the proportional frequencies of the two patterns are visualized in Figs. 5.1 and 5.2, presenting in percentages the proportions of tokens with overt and covert patterns in American English (from COHA) and British English (from the Hansard Corpus), respectively.

Figure 5.1 shows that the covert pattern was rising already in American English in the 1940s and the 1950s with respect to the overt pattern. The normalized frequency of the covert pattern was 0.7 in the 1950s data in COHA, while in that decade there were only two tokens in British English in that decade, with a normalized frequency of zero. In more recent decades the normalized frequencies of the covert pattern were also consis-

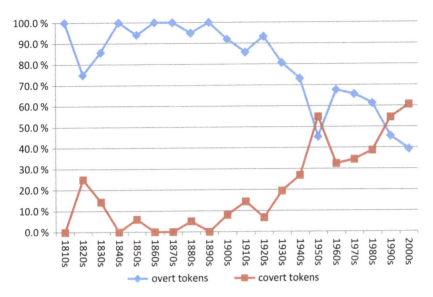

Fig. 5.1 The proportions of overt and covert tokens of *warn* (NP) + *against -ing* in COHA, based on the data in Rudanko and Rickman (2014, 214–215)

tently higher in American English than in British English, and in American English the tokens without an explicit object have outnumbered those of the overt pattern. At the same time even in British English there is a noticeable rise in the frequency of the covert pattern from the 1980s onwards, as can be observed in Fig. 5.2. Overall, the frequencies in Table 5.1 and the proportions of the two patterns in Figs. 5.1 and 5.2 support the idea that the use of the covert pattern is spreading not only in American English but also in British English.

The difference in text type between COHA and the Hansard Corpus should be borne in mind as a caveat, but the data of the present corpora also suggest the working hypothesis that the emergence and the spread of the covert object control pattern was spearheaded by American English, which in turn raises the possibility that the syntactic change in question represents another case of American English influence on British English (on another example of such influence, see for instance Mair and Leech 2006, 327–329). This hypothesis will need to be checked if and when a British equivalent of COHA or an American equivalent of the Hansard Corpus becomes available.

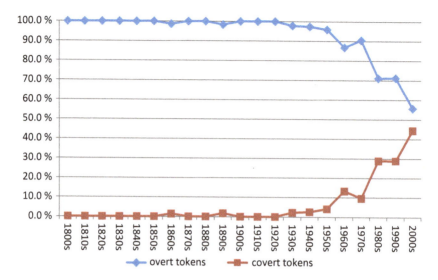

Fig. 5.2 The proportions of overt and covert tokens of *warn* (NP) + *against -ing* in the Hansard Corpus

At this point it is also of interest to raise the question of what may have contributed to the emergence and spread of the covert object control pattern in the system of English predicate complementation in the first place. This change is very much in accordance with general trends favouring gerundial complements that are at the core of the Great Complement Shift (Rohdenburg 2006; Vosberg 2006, 2009), but it may also be recalled that sentential complements in English form a hierarchy of sententiality or nouniness, and that gerundial complements are at the nominal end of the hierarchy in that they are the most nominal type of sentential complement (Ross 2004). Taking this property of gerundial complements into account, it is of interest to consider the incidence of the intransitive non-sentential *against* NP pattern with *warn*, as in *He warned against the decision*.[4] Two examples are given in (7a–b):

(7) a. And as early as 1863, science in the person of Agassiz had warned against extreme courses. (COHA, 1907, MAG)
    b. An editorial in the first issue of Free World warns against the delusion of an easy victory. (COHA, 1941, MAG)

According to Rudanko and Rickman (2014, 215), in the first half of the nineteenth century there was a noticeable increase in the frequency of the non-sentential complementation pattern in COHA, from 3 in the 1900s, to 11 in the 1910s, to 17 in the 1920s and 26 in the 1930s, while the numbers for the sentential pattern lacking an object were lower for each decade. This suggests that the non-sentential pattern paved the way for the sentential pattern without an expressed object.

As for British English, when the search string "[warn].[v*] against" is applied to the data of the Hansard corpus, it is observed that in the nineteenth century the non-sentential covert object pattern was very rare, with only 9 tokens for the whole century. Of more interest is the information for the period from the 1900s to the 1960s. This is given in Table 5.2.

Two examples from British English are given in (8a–b):

(8) a. That is why I am very glad that the Minister of Health recently warned against the dire consequences of any attempt to go back to the idea of a Coalition [...] (Hansard, House of Commons, July 18, 1949)

b. I remind the House that the Jenkins Committee went out of its way to warn against the disclosure of information which, although it might be of interest to those with an inquisitive mind [...] (Hansard, House of Commons, Feb. 21, 1966)

The numbers in Table 5.2 show that in the decades from the 1900s to the 1930s the numbers of the non-sentential covert object pattern continued to be very low, but that there was a noticeable increase in its incidence in the 1940s, to be followed by a sharply rising trend in the 1950s and 1960s.

Table 5.2 Tokens of the non-sentential covert object pattern *warn against* NP in the Hansard Corpus from the 1900s to the 1960s

Decade	Tokens (normalized frequency per million words)
1900s	2 (0.0)
1910s	0 (0.0)
1920s	0 (0.0)
1930s	0 (0.0)
1940s	6 (0.1)
1950s	14 (0.1)
1960s	31 (0.2)

These figures, taken in conjunction with the findings by Rudanko and Rickman (2014) in COHA, reinforce the hypothesis of American influence on British English in this area of grammar. It might be speculated that increased transatlantic contacts in the 1940s and 1950s might have fostered this outcome in those decades. The figures for British English in Table 5.2, taken together with those in Table 5.1, also confirm that the spread of the sentential object control pattern was preceded by the emergence and spread of the non-sentential covert object pattern in British English as it had been in American English.

5.3   THE OCCURRENCE OF OVERT AND COVERT OBJECT CONTROL COMPLEMENTS OF *WARN* IN FIVE REGIONAL VARIETIES

Turning now to the non-core varieties of English in addition to the two core ones, it should be pointed out that no diachronic comparison of the type carried out for American English in Rudanko and Rickman (2014) and for British English above can be contemplated. This is simply because at this time there are no suitable corpora for such a study available for Indian, Pakistani or Philippine English. However, the Global Web-based English corpus (GloWbE) offers a source of information on current usage in these varieties. The corpus is aggregative in nature, and there may be lack of information about the speakers represented, with respect to their status and competence (see Brezina and Meyerhoff 2014; Mukherjee 2015), but its large size nevertheless makes it a valuable tool for investigating Indian, Pakistani or Philippine English.

Considering that the corpus represents present-day English on the Internet, containing texts from blogs and other web sites, the US and Great Britain sections of the corpus are examined as well in order to provide a more comparable picture of the uses of the overt and covert patterns in the two core varieties and the three outer circle varieties. It is worth noting the sizes of the subsections representing the five varieties: the US section contains altogether 386.6 million words of online texts, while the corresponding figures for the GB, India, Pakistan, and Philippines sections are 387.6, 96.4, 51.4, and 43.3, respectively. The sections include texts from general web sites and blogs with a rough 2:1 ratio as regards the word count.

The search string used in the examination of the GloWbE corpus was the same as used with the Hansard Corpus, and again duplicates and irrelevant tokens were excluded from the analysis. Instances of the covert object pattern were attested in the Indian, Pakistani and Philippine subsections, as exemplified in (9a–c):

(9) a. Harsh Neotia of the Bengal Ambuja Group and one of the biggest investors in the state may have a point when he warns against comparing Kolkata with Delhi and Bangalore. (GloWbE-IN, General: "Usual Suspects: Kolkata Past and Present")

b. Accordingly, it is logical to believe that Abdullah ibn Masud warned against recording the Hadith on account of his concern for the general Islamic entity [...] (GloWbE-PK, General: "The Prohibition of Recording the Hadith")

c. Cory, for her part, even warned against resorting to extra-constitutional means to remove Arroyo, even as they themselves had four years earlier ousted Estrada and installed the Illegitimate in her place [...] (GloWbE-PH, General: "President Noynoy Aquino shows he does not have empathy and compassion")

Table 5.3 presents the numbers of tokens of overt and covert object patterns with *warn* (NP) + *against* + V_{ing}, with the normalized frequencies per million words again provided inside parentheses.

As can be observed in Table 5.3, the two core varieties, US and GB, clearly differ from the three outer circle varieties as regards the relationship between the numbers of overt and covert object patterns with *warn*. The figures in the US and GB sections may be regarded as being in line with the results from the recent decades in COHA and the Hansard Corpus,

Table 5.3 The incidence and relative percentages of overt and covert object control constructions with *warn* in five varieties in the GloWbE Corpus (pmw = frequency per million words)

Section	Overt objects (pmw)	%	Covert objects (pmw)	%
US	107 (0.3)	50.0%	107 (0.3)	50.0%
GB	171 (0.4)	52.6%	154 (0.4)	47.4%
PH	27 (0.6)	69.2%	12 (0.3)	30.8%
IN	56 (0.6)	68.3%	26 (0.3)	31.7%
PK	66 (1.3)	65.3%	35 (0.7)	34.7%

showing tokens with covert objects being roughly equal in frequency with those with overt objects. It is worth noting that in the outer circle varieties this is not the case, but that the overt object pattern still prevails—the covert object pattern manifests itself in Indian, Pakistani and Philippine English but its spread obviously lags behind the levels presently seen in American and British English. The difference observed here in the frequencies of the overt and covert object patterns between the US and Philippine English, GB and Indian English, as well as GB and Pakistani English, are statistically significant: levels of statistical significance are observed when analyzing the numbers of tokens with a 2 × 2 Chi Square test on the US and Philippines data (Yates Chi Square, p = 0.0414), the GB and Indian data (Yates Chi Square, p = 0.021) and the GB and Pakistani data (Yates Chi Square, p = 0.0327). It can therefore be concluded that object omission appears to be significantly more common in the examined core varieties of English.

As regards the figures in Table 5.3 further, it is worth noting that the normalized frequencies of the overt object pattern with *warn against -ing* are higher in the outer core varieties, and in Pakistani English, the frequencies per million words are higher for both the overt and covert object patterns. It is possible that the use of *warn* with the *against -ing* complement is generally formal in character, and it can be considered whether the online data on Philippine, Indian and Pakistani English in the GloWbE corpus is stylistically more formal that the texts representing online language in the US and GB sections. In the Pakistani English section of the GloWbE corpus, a large number of the tokens of *warn* (NP) *against -ing* deal with religious issues and doctrines (e.g. "Islam also warns against following in the footsteps of the Shaytaan" (GloWbE-PK, General: "Chapter 3—Muslim Religion Questions and Answers")), and the prominence of texts with this subject matter perhaps explains the higher normalized frequencies of the tokens when compared to the other varieties examined. As noted earlier, the GloWbE subsections include texts from more general web sites as well as blogs, and personal blogs may be assumed to be more informal in their use of language than general web sites. If analyzed separately, the normalized frequencies of the overt and covert tokens with *warn against -ing* are indeed lower in the "blogs only" texts in GloWbE in all four variants examined than in the combination of general web sites and blogs, as seen in Table 5.4:

Table 5.4 The incidence and relative percentages of overt and covert object control constructions with *warn* in five varieties in the GloWbE Corpus (only blogs; pmw = frequency per million words)

Section	Overt objects (pmw)	%	Covert objects (pmw)	%
US	28 (0.2)	45.9%	33 (0.2)	54.1%
GB	44 (0.3)	50.0%	44 (0.3)	50.0%
PH	4 (0.3)	80.0%	1 (0.1)	20.0%
IN	10 (0.4)	66.7%	5 (0.2)	33.3%
PK	11 (0.9)	65.3%	6 (0.5)	34.7%

Comparing the figures in Tables 5.3 and 5.4, it may be possible to see a connection between the frequencies of *warn* (NP) *against -ing* with text type, as the normalized frequencies of *warn* with this complement pattern are lower in texts gleaned from blogs than in both general web sites and blogs together. It might also be tempting to contemplate whether omitting the object is more frequent in text types which are more informal, but the frequencies here may be too low to pursue this question in greater detail.

Given the historical and administrative ties between the United States and the Philippines, one might have expected that of the three outer core varieties, the novel use of the covert object pattern would have been more prominent in Philippine rather than Indian or Pakistani English. The reason for this not being the case in the GloWbE data may have to do with differences in the nature of the texts themselves (as observed earlier, many of the tokens found in the Pakistani data refer to religious doctrines), but it is also possible that differences in the linguistic substrata of India, Pakistan and the Philippines are reflected in the results, the detailed analysis of which is beyond the scope of the present study (for overviews on the influences of indigenous languages on Indian, Pakistani and Philippine English, see e.g. Sedlatschek 2009; Irfan Khan 2012; Schneider 2007, 140–143, respectively). As regards the comparison between Indian and Pakistani English, the proportions of the tokens of overt and covert object patterns are fairly similar. In this respect the results do not fall in line with the general observations made by Shastri (1996), who found Indian English as being closer to Standard Native English (British and American English) as regards the selection of complementation patterns of verbs, nouns, and adjectives, when comparing Indian English corpus data results to findings on Pakistani English made by Baumgardner (1987).

5.4   QUALITATIVE OBSERVATIONS ON THE USE
OF THE COVERT OBJECT PATTERN

In addition to the analysis of the frequencies of *warn against -ing* with overt or covert objects, a number of qualitative observations can be made on the semantic and pragmatic considerations which may play a role in the use of the two patterns. In Rudanko and Rickman (2014) and Chap. 4 of the present volume, attention was given to two dichotomies in the interpretation of the covert objects, following the discussion in Huddleston and Pullum (2002, 303) of unexpressed human objects with selected classes of verbs. Using the verb *please* as an example, they observe that some verbs which select unexpressed human objects "appear more readily in intransitives when the situation is habitual or unactualized—e.g. *He never fails to please, I'll aim to please,* but hardly ?*His behavior at lunch pleased*" (Huddleston and Pullum 2002, 303). The verb *warn* was not listed by Huddleston and Pullum in same class of verbs in this regard alongside *please*, but interpretations of the covert object control pattern with *warn* may be examined on the basis of this observation. Firstly, it could be asked whether the understood, implicit object is specific or general in character. Secondly, as regards the kind of situation expressed in the lower clause of the construction, the habituality or regularity of the action being described can be examined, as well as if the action is actualized or unactualized.

In Rudanko and Rickman (2014), it was suggested that with the verb *warn*, the unactualized and 'irrealis' nature of the activities or processes described in the lower clause might be connected with the possibility of omitting the matrix object. These features of the lower clause, which on the basis of the observation by Huddleston and Pullum are typical of a reduced degree of transitivity, are indeed characteristic of the kinds of actions that one would usually warn someone against doing. Objectless instances of *warn against -ing* are also found in the GloWbE data with unactualized, 'irrealis' interpretations of the lower clause, as in (10a–c):

(10) a. While several Western nations have supported Israel's military offensive and its "right to defense", they have warned against launching a ground invasion of Gaza enclave. (GloWbE-IN, General: "Egypt says raids would end; death toll in Gaza 122—World—DNA")

   b. Dreams about himself guided John Bosco's vocation, e.g., the
      decisive first dream and one during his late teen years that
      warned against entering a certain Franciscan monastery.
      (GloWbE-PH, General: "The Dreams of St John Bosco")
   c. Panetta said the Pentagon "has to play a role in trying to be
      able to achieve fiscal responsibility," but warned against allow-
      ing the cuts, which would take place as a result of the failure to
      reach a deficit reduction deal last year. (GloWbE-PK, General:
      "Defence cuts would be 'disastrous' for US")

However, some instances can also be found where the action expressed in
the lower clause can be interpreted as having occurred, as exemplified
in (11a–b):

(11) a. The federal government warns against talking on a cellphone
        while driving, but no state legislature has banned it.
        (GloWbE-US, General: "Driven to Distraction")
     b. Other activists have warned against continuing state-sponsored
        violence, after mass arrests of Rohingya men were reported in
        the north of the state. (GloWbE-PK, General: "Burma
        Massacre and the silence of the world")

In (11a), it is evident that the practice of talking on a cellphone while driv-
ing had already taken place by some members of the public before the
federal government's warning. In some instances, the lower clause verb
itself indicates the actualization of the process, as seen with the verb *con-
tinue* in (11b). In fact, occasionally the borderline between 'realis' and
'irrealis' interpretations may be fuzzy: in the earlier example sentence (9c),
it is suggested that "resorting to extra-constitutional means" had been
earlier done by people in power who now hypocritically warn others of
doing something similar. If, however, the lower level clause is to be strictly
analyzed in relation to the removal of Arroyo, the action had not taken
place previously. Examples such as these make it challenging to conduct a
quantitative analysis of the actualized versus irrealis dichotomy, but in the
majority of the tokens the irrealis interpretation seems relevant.
   The other dichotomy involves the semantic characteristics of the overt
or covert object. In his discussion of the covert objects, Rizzi (1986) puts
some emphasis on the interpretation of the covert object being general
rather than specific. The dichotomy between specific versus general objects

is also mentioned by Huddleston and Pullum (2002, 303), who observe that the implicit objects of intransitive verbs may be of both types. It is therefore interesting to examine the nature of the overt as well as covert objects with *warn against -ing* in the four varieties of the GloWbE corpus. An analysis of the tokens with an overt object shows that the objects can be quite specific, naming or identifying the persons who are or were warned, as in (12a) below, or more general, as in (12b):

(12) a. Thankfully in the 1960s those well-meaning, floral-printed matrons already existed, surely the same ones as warned my mother in the early millennium against allowing my brother and I to read Harry Potter […] (GloWbE-US, Blog: "In Which We Unwrinkle The Nature Of Time")

b. I'm not an attorney, and I can't give legal advice, but there are some very simple legal terms you need to follow. You can't have someone give a testimonial for a product that doesn't exist. You have to deliver within a certain time frame. I just want to warn people against saying, "Yes, this is intuitive. It makes sense. Now I'm going to go and do it. I'm going to throw up one survey." (GloWbE-US, Blog: "How To Get Tons Of People To Tell You The EXACT Product They're Desperate To Buy From You ... And THEN 'Pre-Buy' It BEFORE You Create It")

In (12b), we can observe that the object does not refer to any specifically identified individual or group of individuals, but the warning is given to any person who would potentially find oneself in a similar situation. There are also instances where the overt object may be seen as representing an intermediate level as far as specificity or generality is concerned. For example, object NPs such as *locals, the audience*, and *parents* limit the reference to a subset of people rather than the general public, but nevertheless specific individual people are not necessarily explicitly identified.

With covert objects, the interpretation of the understood object can likewise be specific or general, as seen in examples (13a–d):

(13) a. Sam shook his head; his heart wanting to believe... but his instincts warning against trusting a demon (GloWbE-US, General: "Fanfic: Tidings of Great Joy, Supernatural")

     b. He also reminded Sereno to remain faithful to the Constitutions and warned against overstepping the mandate to interpret the law (GloWbE-PH, General: "Binay urges new chief justice to be interpreter, not maker, of the law")

     c. Pharmacists warn against buying prescriptions online, as well as picking them up at different locations. (GloWbE-US, General: "9 Things Your Pharmacist Wants to Tell You—Woman's Day")

     d. Hebrews 6:4–6, warns against falling away from the faith ... (GloWbE-US, General: "OCA—Q & A—Hebrews 6:4–6—Falling Away from the Faith")

In examples (13a–d), the interpretation of the unexpressed objects appears rather clear. In (13a), the understood object appears to be Sam himself, in (13b) the object is Sereno. In (13c) and (13d), the warnings are targeted to people in general, or perhaps the subsets of the public consisting of buyers of prescription medicine and people of faith. However, instances like (13a–b) where the object of *warn* can be interpreted as referring to a single individual person are rare in the data examined. In fact, in the US subsection of the GloWbE corpus there are only two cases among the 107 covert objects found with *warn against -ing* where the object can be understood as unequivocally referring to a specific individual. In comparison, as many as 31 out of 107 overt objects in the same data were NPs with a reference to a single person (such as *me*, *Galileo*, *Bond*, and *Romney*).[5] The GB section of GloWbE shows a similar tendency, with 64 out of 171 overt objects denoting specific individuals, while only five of the 154 covert objects can be interpreted in this way. In the Indian English material, 11 out of the 56 overt objects referred to a single person, and in the Pakistani English material, this was the likewise the case with 11 out of 66 overt objects, while none of the covert objects found in the Indian and Pakistani data had this kind of reference. In the Philippine English data there were two tokens of overt and covert objects each with a single person reference. It therefore appears that the dichotomy of specific versus general is a relevant characteristic in the usage of the covert object control pattern with *warn*.

    In Rudanko and Rickman (2014), it was speculated that one factor that may have contributed to the spread of the covert object control pattern especially in political discourse is the fact that the interpretation of the understood object is occasionally vague or indeterminate. (For the concept of indeterminacy in connection with omitted objects, see also Eu

2017.) As was noted in cases such as (13a–b), the understood object is not indeterminate, but the idea of indeterminacy does have relevance to some tokens in the current data. In such cases the speaker expresses caution about a potential threat without directing the warning to any specific entity. Two cases in point are given in (14a–b):

(14) a. After the deaths, Nick Clegg also warned against arming police. "I don't think this is the time to rush to instant judgments; this really is a time for mourning and support, of course, for the family and friends of the two women who have been killed," the deputy prime minister said. (GloWbE-GB, General: "Police should not be routinely armed, says Theresa May")

   b. On August 4, Brent Scowcroft, who had been national security adviser to the first President Bush, went on Sunday television to warn against attacking Saddam. (GloWbE-US, General: "THE IRAQ WAR—PART II: Was There Even a Decision?")

To consider example (14a), the understood object of *warn* may be interpreted as referring generally to political actors who might contemplate taking action towards arming police, but this is not necessarily the only possible interpretation. The words may also have been directed at the media, whose reporting of tragic events is often crucial in shaping public opinion and directing the discourse that follows such event. A similar interpretation is also applicable to (14b). Thus the omission of the object leaves it open who exactly the warning is aimed at, which may in some circumstances be an attractive option. The reason is that the speaker is able to make use of the indeterminacy of the construction, thus avoiding the potentially face-threatening act of directly naming the target of the warning.

5.5   Concluding Remarks

The investigation into the occurrence of overt and covert object patterns with *warn* (NP) *against -ing* has shown that in American and British English, two core varieties of the language, the proportions of the covert tokens have come closer to those of the overt tokens in the last couple of decades. The tokens of the two patterns in COHA and the Hansard Corpus could be interpreted as showing that the increase of the covert object pattern began earlier in American English, but more conclusive observations would require more comparable corpora as regards their structure and subject matter. However, the rise of the covert object pattern in both diachronic corpora is clear. It is possible to assume that the non-core varieties have yet to develop along similar lines, and the study of the relevant tokens in five varieties included in the GloWbE corpus indeed provides support for this assumption. As regards the study of Bach's Generalization, the results in this regard shed light on the matter from a new perspective, and the examination of different kinds of varieties of English promise interesting prospects for further study.

In addition to quantitative analysis of the corpus data, this study examines the interpretation of covert objects from a qualitative point of view. The findings corroborate ideas expressed by Rizzi (1986) in that covert objects were frequently found to have a general interpretation, in line with the emphasis placed on such interpretations by Rizzi. At the same time, the data also revealed that sometimes, though less often, covert objects can refer to specific entities. Furthermore, certain pragmatic considerations may be relevant as regards the use of the covert pattern, as the indeterminacy of the unexpressed object may at times be a desirable or attractive characteristic of the pattern. Such qualitative analyses likewise appear to warrant closer study in the future, in connection with the verb *warn* as well as other semantically similar verbs.

NOTES

1. There are in fact some speakers of English who are less than happy about the status of sentence (1b), and it seems clear that the frequency of this type of sentence with *promise* has been decreasing in English (see Rohdenburg 2006). However, sentences of the type of (1b) are found easily enough even in recent corpora. The sentences in (ia–b) are illustrations.

   (i) a. He drank a lot, but he'd promised her to slow down. (COCA, 1990, FIC)
   b. "My little sis-ter's sick, and she likes your rabbits so much that I promised her to come and ask your father for permission to pet them sometimes." (COCA, 1993, FIC)

   Because of such authentic tokens, the present authors do not contest Bach's assumption that (1b) is well formed.

2. Most work on detransitivization, including Groefsema (1995) and García Velasco and Portero Muñoz (2002), has focused on understood objects in

simple sentences, without reference to Bach's Generalization. In contrast, the present chapter deals with covert objects in object control sentences. From another perspective, it should be noted with respect to sentential complementation that in addition to detransitivization processes in English, transitivization processes should also be recognized. For instance, creative or innovative uses of the transitive *into -ing* pattern may involve transitivization (see for instance Rudanko 2015, Chap. 7; Kim and Davies 2016).

3. Rickman and Rudanko (2018) also investigated the construction in more than half of the decades of the Hansard Corpus, though with a somewhat different search string. In spite of the difference in search strings, the overall results are largely similar when the results for the decades that they investigated are compared with the present findings. The present study also covers the decades that were not considered by Rickman and Rudanko (2018).

4. We thank an anonymous reviewer for pointing to this line of investigation.

5. It is worth noting that plural object NPs can of course also refer to specific and clearly determinable groups of people (e.g. *member of the US Congress*); however, the analysis of overt singular NP objects and similar types of covert object referents can be regarded as allowing a clearer insight into one aspect of the specific versus general dichotomy of the understood objects.

References

Bach, Emmon. 1980. In Defense of Passive. *Linguistics and Philosophy* 3: 297–341.

Baumgardner, Robert J. 1987. Utilising Pakistani English Newspaper to Teach Grammar. *World Englishes* 6 (3): 241–252.

Brezina, Vaclav, and Miriam Meyerhoff. 2014. Significant or Random? A Critical Review of Sociolinguistic Generalizations Based on Large Corpora. *International Journal of Corpus Linguistics* 19: 1–28.

Chomsky, Noam. 1981. *Lectures on Government and Binding*. Dordrecht: Foris.

———. 1986. *Knowledge of Language: Nature, Origin, and Use*. New York: Praeger.

Eu, Jinseung. 2017. On the Nature of Object Omission: Indefiniteness as Indeterminacy. *English Language and Linguistics* 22 (3): 523–530.

García Velasco, Daniel, and Carmen Portero Muñoz. 2002. Understood Objects in Functional Grammar. *Web Papers in Functional Grammar* 76. http://home.hum.uva.nl/fg/working_artcis/WPFG76.pdf.

Groefsema, Marjolein. 1995. Understood Arguments: A Semantic/Pragmatic Approach. *Lingua* 96: 139–161.

Huddleston, Rodney, and Geoffrey K. Pullum. 2002. *The Cambridge Grammar of the English Language*. Cambridge: Cambridge University Press.

Irfan Khan, H. 2012. The Evolution of Pakistani English (PakE) as a Legitimate Variety of English. *International Journal of Applied Linguistics & English Literature* 1 (5): 90–99.

Jespersen, Otto. [1940] 1961. *A Modern English Grammar on Historical Principles. Part V: Syntax*. Vol. IV. Reprinted 1961. London and Copenhagen: George Allen and Unwin/Ejnar Munksgaard.

Kim, Jong-Bok, and Mark Davies. 2016. The *INTO*-CAUSATIVE Construction in English: A Construction-Based Perspective. *English Language and Linguistics* 20: 55–83.

Landau, Idan. 2013. *Control in Generative Grammar. A Research Companion*. Cambridge: Cambridge University Press.

Mair, Christian, and Geoffrey Leech. 2006. Current Changes in English Syntax. In *The Handbook of English Linguistics*, ed. B. Aarts and A. McMahon, 328–342. Malden, MA: Wiley-Blackwell.

Mukherjee, Joybrato. 2015. Response to Mark Davies and Robert Fuchs. *English World-Wide* 36: 34–37.

Rickman, Paul, and Juhani Rudanko. 2018. *Corpus-Based Studies on Non-Finite Complements in Recent English*. London: Palgrave Macmillan.

Rizzi, Luigi. 1986. Null Objects in Italian and the Theory of Pro. *Linguistic Inquiry* 17 (3): 501–557.

Rohdenburg, Günter. 2006. The Role of Functional Constraints in the Evolution of the English Complementation System. In *Syntax, Style and Grammatical Norms: English from 1500–2000*, ed. Christine Dalton-Puffer, Dieter Kastovsky, Nicholas Ritt, and Herbert Schendl, 143–166. Bern: Peter Lang.

Ross, John R. 2004. Nouniness. In *Fuzzy Grammar*, ed. B. Aarts, D. Denison, E. Keizer, and G. Popova, 351–422. Oxford: Oxford University Press.

Rudanko, Juhani. 2015. *Linking Form and Meaning: Studies on Selected Control Patterns in Recent English*. Basingstoke: Palgrave Macmillan.

Rudanko, Juhani, and Paul Rickman. 2014. Null Objects and Sentential Complements, with Evidence from the Corpus of Historical American English. In *Corpus Interrogation and Grammatical Patterns*, ed. K. Davidse, C. Gentens, L. Ghesquière, and L. Vandelanotte, 209–221. Amsterdam: John Benjamins.

Schneider, Edgar. 2007. *Postcolonial English: Varieties Around the World*. Cambridge: Cambridge University Press.

Sedlatschek, Andreas. 2009. *Contemporary Indian English: Variation and Change*. Amsterdam and Philadelphia: John Benjamins.

Shastri, S.V. 1996. Using Computer Corpora in the Description of Language with Special Reference to Complementation in Indian English. In *South Asian English: Structure, Use, and Users*, ed. R. Baumgardner, 70–81. Urbana: University of Illinois Press.

Vosberg, Uwe. 2006. *Die Grosse Komplementverschiebung*. Tübingen: Narr.

———. 2009. Non-Finite Complements. In *One Language, Two Grammars? Differences Between British and American English*, ed. Günter Rohdenburg and Julia Schlüter, 212–227. Cambridge: Cambridge University Press. https://doi.org/10.1017/CBO9780511551970.012.

CHAPTER 6

New Light on *-Ing* Complements of *Prevent,* with Recent Data from Large Corpora

Abstract This chapter examines the two types of *-ing* complements with the matrix verb *prevent*, where the verb is followed by an object NP and an *-ing* complement with or without the preposition *from*. The alternation is of interest for instance because it has been observed in earlier work that the non-prepositional pattern is much more frequent in British English than in American English, with the difference constituting a major grammatical difference between the two major core varieties of English. The present study sheds new light on aspects of the variation between the two alternants with very recent data from large electronic corpora, such as the NOW Corpus. In addition to observing differences between British and American English, the study extends the range of data to Indian, Pakistani and Philippine English to gain a view of the variation, or lack of it, in these varieties of the language. Going beyond descriptive objectives, the study also examines the question of what factors may promote the incidence of the non-prepositional pattern. The study furthermore investigates whether new data may shed fresh light on the two types of constructions from the point of view of the distinction between control and NP Movement.

Keywords Complementation • Corpus linguistics • NP movement • Object control • Regional variation

© The Author(s) 2019
M. Kaunisto, J. Rudanko, *Variation in Non-finite Constructions in English*, https://doi.org/10.1007/978-3-030-19044-6_6

6.1   Introduction

This chapter is about a specific aspect of complementation in recent varieties of English. The outstanding feature of complementation concerns licensing. The licensing property establishes a relationship summed up concisely by Huddleston and Pullum (2002):

> The most important property of complements in clause structure is that they require the presence of an appropriate verb that **licenses** them (Huddleston and Pullum 2002, 219; for the related notion of a theta grid, see Carnie 2007, 223)

Of course, adjectives and nouns can also license complements, but the licensing property establishes a relationship of mutual dependence between the licensing constituent—which may be called the head of the construction—and the complement that is licensed by the head. In English a single head may often license more than one type of complement. Sometimes the type of complement selected by a head may depend on a particular sense of a head. To take a simple example, we may consider the verb *boast*. Its senses include "speak vaingloriously, extol oneself; to vaunt, brag *of*, *about*, glory *in*" (sense 2 in the *OED*), and "possess as a thing to be proud of, to have to show" (sense 7 in the *OED*). As indicated in the entry, the first of these senses may be linked to prepositional complements introduced by *of* or *about*, but the second is linked to NP complements, as is clear in illustrations of the sense, as in *The clematic, the favoured flower, Which boasts the name of virgin-bower* (1810, Scott, *Lady of the Lake*).

While the complement selection properties of a head may be linked to particular senses of the head, it is also often the case in English that the sense of the head may remain fairly constant even when the verb licenses more than one type of complement. In this case it is of interest to consider the incidence of the alternating constructions for instance in different regional varieties of English and to examine variation between the variants from a diachronic perspective. Further, it is relevant to inquire into the syntax and semantics of the alternating variants. The present study seeks to contribute to this area of research. The focus is on non-finite complements of the matrix verb *prevent*.

To introduce the constructions selected by *prevent* to be examined in this chapter, consider the sentences in (1a–b), from the NOW Corpus:

(1) a. Denauer stuck to Coutinho like glue and prevented him from pulling the strings. (NOW, GB, 2016, *Liverpool Echo*)

   b. ... police deployed a taser device against a man armed with a large bladed knife, preventing him cutting the throat of a stranger ... (NOW, GB, 2016, *Glasgow Evening Times*)

In both (1a–b) the matrix verb *prevent* selects a sentential *-ing* complement, with an object NP intervening between the verb and the *-ing* clause. In (1a) the complement construction also includes the preposition *from*, and it may be labelled the "NP *from -ing*" pattern and in (1b) complement it is non-prepositional and may be labelled "NP *-ing*."

This chapter has two main objectives. The first objective is to investigate the incidence of the two types of non-finite complements of *prevent* in a number of regional varieties on English. These varieties include British and American English, and in addition, three non-core varieties, Indian, Pakistani and Philippine English are also considered. It has been observed in earlier work that the NP *-ing* construction with *prevent* is a feature of British English and tends to be much rarer in American English (Mair 2002), and here the goal is to find out if this expectation is confirmed in the present dataset. Assuming that such earlier work is confirmed in the data considered, it is also of interest to inquire into the presence or absence of the type of variation in question between the two patterns in non-core varieties, because such a study may shed light on the impact of British and American English on non-core varieties. It may be added that the study of complementation in non-core varieties with data from large electronic corpora has been attracting increasing attention in recent years (see, for instance, Mukherjee 2003; Mukherjee and Hoffmann 2006; Mukherjee and Schilk 2008; Schilk et al. 2012, 2013; Bernaisch et al. 2014; Deshors 2015; Deshors and Gries 2016),[1] and the comments on non-core varieties here are offered as a contribution to this emerging area of research. As regards the selection of the non-core varieties in the study, all of them represent varieties on the Asian continent, but Indian and Pakistani English have cultural and historical ties to British English,[2] whereas Philippine English has historical connections with American English. From this perspective, it is interesting to examine the usage of the constructions under study in these varieties in relation to the current situation in the core varieties.

The second objective is to inquire into the grammatical and derivational properties of the types of constructions selected by the matrix verb *prevent* that are exemplified in (1a–b). To examine the grammatical and derivational properties in question, essential use is made of corpus evidence.

The NOW Corpus (News on the Web; https://corpus.byu.edu/now) serves as an important source of data in both parts of this investigation. It is a large corpus consisting of texts from web-based newspapers and magazines representing 20 different regional varieties of English, and it is updated on a daily basis. At the beginning of April 2018, the corpus contained approximately 5.9 billion words of text from 2010 to April 2018. Because of its size, clearly defined structure, and because it enables one to investigate usage in different regional varieties, it is a suitable source of data for work on the two objectives outlined. To gain information on specific questions relating to diachronic developments in the use of the two constructions and on the grammatical properties of the variants, the Hansard Corpus and the Corpus of Historical American English (COHA), were consulted as well.

6.2   THE NP *FROM -ING* AND NP *-ING* COMPLEMENT CONSTRUCTIONS IN SELECTED REGIONAL VARIETIES OF ENGLISH

In order to examine both the occurrence and degree of present-day variation between the "NP *from -ing*" and "NP *-ing*" patterns with the matrix verb *prevent* in the two core varieties, American and British English, and three non-core varieties, Indian, Pakistani and Philippine English, the NOW Corpus provides a wealth of data for in-depth study. For the purpose of comparing the use of the two patterns in the five regional varieties, the search was limited to only those tokens with a third person singular accusative pronoun, the search query being "[prevent].[v*] him|her|it". As a result, this query produced tokens of the different inflectional forms of the verb *prevent* immediately followed by one of the object pronouns. The search string was selected in order to abstract away the potential influence of the Complexity Principle (Rohdenburg 1996), which would associate a complex object NP with the more explicit NP *from -ing* variant. Furthermore, the searches were limited to the latter half of the year 2016, i.e. beginning from July 1, 2016, and ending on December 31, 2016. The search results were then manually examined and categorized on the basis of whether the tokens represented instances where *prevent* selects a sentential complement as in examples (1a–b) or not. With this simple search query, some of the search results are either irrelevant from the point of view of the present study or were otherwise chosen to be excluded from the analysis. Illustrations are given in (2a–c).

(2) a. There is no vaccine against Zika virus. The best way to prevent it is to avoid mosquito bites, especially when traveling to areas with active outbreaks […] (NOW, US, 2016, *KBZK Bozeman News*)
b. Minor's mother said she went downstairs in an effort to "prevent her daughter from getting inside," but she was able to get inside. (NOW, US, 2016, fox6now.com)
c. They say it came as a shock when they saw the rates skyrocket and feel as if the County Commissioners did nothing to prevent it from happened. (NOW, US, 2016, Firstcoastnews.com)

In example (2a), the verb *prevent* simply selects a noun phrase object with no further sentential complement. The case in example (2b), on the other hand, is undoubtedly an example of the "NP *from -ing*" pattern. However, instead of the pronoun *her* constituting the entire NP in its own right, the pronoun functions as the modifier to the head of the NP *daughter*. Since the principle of limiting the data was made with the intention to examine only instances with a single pronoun NP, the relatively few tokens such as the ones in (2b) were excluded from the study. Example (2c) represents a third type of token likewise left out of the analysis. Here we have an erroneous verb form, with *happening* most likely intended instead of *happened*. Although one might be able to make an educated guess as to the form intended, these tokens were omitted from further study.

After excluding unwanted tokens among the search results, the remaining tokens were examined as to whether they represented the "NP *from -ing*" or "NP *-ing*" construction. Instances of both types of constructions were found in all five regional varieties. Examples (3a–f) represent relevant tokens of the two constructions as found in the three non-core varieties examined:

(3) a. Squeeze half a lemon while preparing rice and it will prevent it from sticking. (NOW, IN, 2016, *Times of India*)
b. What an inquiry could do, surely, is something more modest, but very important. It could study what State and non-State institutions in the wake of real child abuse scandals, of which

there have been all too many, are doing to prevent it happening again. (NOW, IN, *The New Indian Express*)

c. Meanwhile, the puppet authorities continued to place Syed Ali Gilani under house arrest to prevent him from leading the demonstrations. (NOW, PK, 2016, *Pakistan Observer*)

d. He returned to play and later on complained about cramps in his left and right calf that prevented him bowling further in the match. (NOW, PK, 2016, *Pakistan Observer*)

e. The agents also prevented her from leaving when she tried to go to her car to get her identification card. (NOW, PH, 2016, *InterAksyon*)

f. Duterte had turned the tables on her by saying she had allowed her "weakness"—specifically, a supposed romantic liaison with a driver-bodyguard who dealt with the prison groups involved in the drug trade—to prevent her taking tough action as a DOJ chief should have done […] (NOW, PH, 2016, *InterAksyon*)

Table 6.1 below presents both the absolute frequencies and the normalized frequencies of the two constructions in the five regional varieties studied in the NOW Corpus. It is worth noting that the sizes of the datasets, i.e., texts from July–December of 2016, in the varieties, with the word count of the GB data being 84.9 million words, and that of the US, IN, PK, and PH sections being 92.3M, 110.6M, 31.7M, and 35.3M words, respectively.

The results seen in Table 6.1 are in line with the observations made by Mair (2002, 2009, 274) as regards the difference between British and American English: in the GB section of the NOW Corpus, the construction without the preposition *from* is proportionally notably more frequent

Table 6.1 The frequencies of *prevent* NP *from -ing* and *prevent* NP *-ing* in five sections of the NOW Corpus, July–December 2016 (pmw = per million words)

	NP from -ing *(pmw)*	%	*NP* -ing *(pmw)*	%
GB (Great Britain)	326 (3.8)	66%	168 (2.0)	34%
US (United States)	422 (4.6)	97%	13 (0.1)	3%
IN (India)	298 (2.7)	97%	10 (0.1)	3%
PK (Pakistan)	87 (2.7)	93%	7 (0.2)	7%
PH (Philippines)	152 (4.3)	97%	4 (0.1)	3%

than it is in the corresponding section representing American English. The statistical difference between the frequencies of the two constructions in the two varieties is significant (Chi Square = 139.9, df = 1; p < 0.0001). An observation further underlining the rareness of the "NP *-ing*" construction with *prevent* in American English can be made in the few occurrences found in the US data, as three of the 13 tokens found were in texts gleaned from CNN International, *Newsweek*, and Deutsche Welle, whose reporters may include people from around the world.

As regards the non-core varieties, the ratios of the two constructions largely resemble the situation seen in American English, with only a few tokens found of the *prevent* NP *-ing* pattern. No major difference is seen between Indian, Pakistani and Philippine English. Interestingly, the constructions without *from* are not particularly frequent in Indian and Pakistani English. Considering the historical connections between these varieties with British English, this finding makes it desirable to consider the diachronic changes in the use of the two constructions. Mair and Leech (2006) observe that the variant lacking *from* with *prevent* was attested in both British and American English, but that it has disappeared in American English in the twentieth century.

In order to shed light on the diachronic occurrences of the two patterns in the course of the last two hundred years in British English, the instances of "prevent him|her|it" were searched in the Hansard Corpus, containing transcripts of the speeches given in the British parliament between 1803 and 2005. A brief survey was conducted on the frequencies of the two constructions over periods of two years in 25-year intervals, i.e., 1850–51, 1875–76, 1900–01, 1925–26, 1950–51, 1975–76, and 2000–01. The results of the survey are presented in Table 6.2 and Fig. 6.1 below.

Table 6.2 The frequencies of *prevent* NP *from -ing* and *prevent* NP *-ing* in the Hansard Corpus

	NP from -ing	%	NP -ing	%
1850–51	65	86%	11	14%
1875–76	50	69%	22	31%
1900–01	26	35%	48	65%
1925–26	55	45%	66	55%
1950–51	83	72%	33	28%
1975–76	124	78%	34	22%
2000–01	107	74%	37	26%

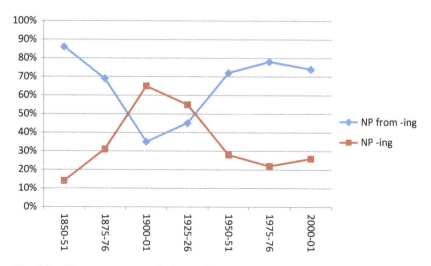

Fig. 6.1   The percentages of tokens of *prevent* NP *from -ing* and *prevent* NP *-ing* in the Hansard Corpus

Examples of both constructions in the Hansard data are given in (4a–d):

(4) a. Various causes had prevented him from introducing the subject at an earlier period of the session, [...] (Hansard, House of Commons, July 23, 1850)

    b. If we are exporting arms to Zaire are there implemented reservations to prevent her from supplying those arms to any of the forces in Angola? (Hansard, House of Lords, Oct. 22, 1975)

    c. If he thought the measure was right or just, no fear of agitation or opposition would prevent him giving it his support [...] (Hansard, House of Commons, Mar. 24, 1851)

    d. The noble Baroness also asked whether the legislation on drinking in public places prevent her having a drink with her family [...] (Hansard, House of Lords, Apr. 2, 2001)

As can be seen in Table 6.2 and the illustration in Fig. 6.1, instances of the "*prevent* NP *-ing*" pattern were indeed found in the nineteenth century data, and in the Hansard Corpus, tokens of this pattern even outnumbered those of its rival construction with *from* in the 1900–01 and 1925–26 datasets. Therefore the occurrence of the pattern clearly cannot be regarded as one that would have been developed in British English after the independence of India and Pakistan, which might have explained the lower numbers of the occurrences of the NP *-ing* pattern in Indian and Pakistani English today in comparison with British English. Nevertheless, it is also interesting to observe that the pattern with *from* has become more frequent in the Hansard Corpus towards the present day, and the ratios between the frequencies of the two constructions are close to those seen in the GB section of the NOW Corpus.[3]

Considering the "*prevent* NP *-ing*" pattern in American English, more light can be shed on the issue by examining the occurrences of the two constructions at similar 25-year intervals in the Corpus of Historical American English (COHA), again with "[prevent].[v*] him|her|it" as the search query. The results are presented in Table 6.3 and Fig. 6.2 below.

Although the numbers of tokens in the COHA data are relatively small, it can clearly be observed that throughout the last 150 years, the NP *from* *-ing* pattern has been more frequent than the NP *-ing* pattern with the verb *prevent*. Illustrations of the two patterns are given in examples (5a–d):

(5) a. His position at court did not prevent him from bestowing much time and pains on the education of Sophie, for many years his only child. (COHA, MAG, 1862)
  b. Her face flushed from the heat, she sat on the unmade bed as though to prevent him from returning there. (COHA, FIC, 1993)
  c. He put his hands on her shoulders, and prevented her rising, for just then he was unwilling she should see his countenance, which he feared would betray the suffering he was resolved to conceal. (COHA, FIC, 1875)

Table 6.3 The frequencies of *prevent* NP *from -ing* and *prevent* NP *-ing* in the Corpus of Historical American English

	NP from -ing	%	NP -ing	%
1850–51	30	97%	1	3%
1875–76	30	77%	9	23%
1900–01	17	81%	4	19%
1925–26	12	75%	4	25%
1950–51	18	100%	0	0%
1975–76	28	93%	2	7%
2000–01	25	96%	1	4%

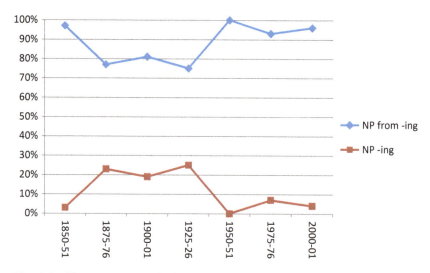

Fig. 6.2   The percentages of tokens of *prevent* NP *from -ing* and *prevent* NP *-ing* in COHA

> d. There was a bend halfway up, which prevented him seeing to the top; round the corner a light was burning, but there seemed to be no-one around; so he began to make his way slowly to where he could see round the corner. (COHA, FIC, 1975)

The numbers of the NP *-ing* pattern are perhaps too small here to say anything conclusive on the weakening of the pattern over the years, but the clear preference of the NP *from -ing* pattern in the most recent dataset (2000–01) in COHA over its rival construction matches that seen in the NOW Corpus in Table 6.1.

6.3   On the Grammatical Analysis of NP *from -ing* and NP *-ing* Complement Constructions of *Prevent*

The objective in this section is to consider the basic theoretical question of how the two constructions should be analyzed syntactically. This is of initial interest because there is an apparent discrepancy between two widely recognized approaches to their analysis in the established literature. Postal (1974) analyzes *prevent* as what is termed an N-verb, illustrating the point with the sentence *I prevented the nurse from moving the patient*, and commenting that the post-verbal NP, *the nurse*, is a "derived" constituent of the main clause. Postal goes on to state the "only viable account of this derivation involves Raising operation into superordinate object position" (Postal 1974, 261). Setting the technicalities of the movement operation aside here, the point is that the derivation thus involves a type of NP Movement, which may be called Subject to Object Raising, to use a suitably descriptive term from Postal's framework. In this approach *prevent*, at least when it selects the NP *from -ing* construction, is thus analyzed as an NP Movement or Subject to Object Raising verb.

The other analysis is best exemplified by Sag and Pollard (1991). They proceed from some important methodological considerations offered originally by Radford (1981). Radford pointed to the well-known contrast between *persuade*, as in *John persuaded Bill PRO to leave* (59d in Radford 1981) and *promise*, as in *John promised Bill PRO to leave* (59e in Radford 1981), where PRO represents the understood pronominal subject of the infinitive in both sentences, but where *persuade* involves object control and *promise* involves subject control. That is, in the sentence with *persuade* the understood lower subject is interpreted as coreferential with the higher object and in the sentence with *promise* the understood lower subject is interpreted as coreferential with the higher subject. Radford notes that a "yet-to-be-developed Theory of Control" would be desirable to predict whether a higher verb is a subject control or an object control verb, and goes on:

> Pending the development of such a theory, it would seem necessary simply to specify in the lexical entry for verbs like *persuade* or *promise* whether they are subject control or nonsubject-control verbs. This is unsatisfactory as a solution to the control problem, however, for a number of reasons. Firstly, arbitrary lists of properties associated with properties have no predictive or explanatory value: ask the question 'How do you know this is a verb of subject control?', and you get the non-answer 'Because it's listed as a verb of subject control in the Lexicon.' Secondly, treating control (of PRO) as a lexically governed phenomenon implies that control properties are entirely arbitrary, and hence will vary in random fashion from dialect to dialect, or language to language: this would lead us to expect that the counterpart of:
>
> (62) John persuaded Bill PRO to leave ...
>
> in some other dialect or language would have subject control rather than nonsubject control (i.e. would have PRO interpreted as referring to *John* rather than to *Bill*). But as far as we know, this is not the case. (Radford 1981, 381)

For their part, Sag and Pollard (1991, 65) provide a list of object control verbs which includes *order, persuade, bid, charge, command, direct, enjoin, instruct, advise, authorize, mandate, encourage, impel, induce,* and *influence,* to take the first 15 of them. It should be added that *prevent,* given as *prevent (from),* is also included in the list. They then suggest that such verbs exhibit a semantic regularity and can be characterized as verbs of the *order/permit* type. They write:

> Verbs of the *order/permit* type all submit to a semantic analysis involving STATES OF AFFAIRS (SOAs) where a certain participant (the referent of the object) is influenced by another participant (the referent of the subject) to perform an action ... The influencing participant maybe an agent (as in *Kim persuaded Sandy to leave*) or a nonagent (as in *Ignorance of thermodynamics compelled Pat to enroll in a poetry class*). The semantics of all verbs in this class thus involves a soa whose relation is of the INFLUENCE type. With respect to such soas, we may identify three semantic roles, which we will refer to as INFLUENCE (the possibly agentive influencer), INFLUENCED (the typically animate participant influenced by the influence) and SOA-ARG (the action that the influenced participant is influenced to perform) (or, in the case of verbs like *prevent* and *forbid,* not to perform). (Sag and Pollard 1991, 66)

Prevent (from) is included in the list of object control verbs in Sag and Pollard (1991, 65), and *prevent* is also specifically mentioned in the quotation given. Regarding the semantic analysis presented for object control verbs, it is based on the notions of influencing in the Sag and Pollard analysis, with the referent of the subject (in an active sentence) influencing the referent of the object not to perform the action expressed by the state of affairs argument. (The notion of influencing seems close to the notion of "acting on": the referent of the subject acts on the referent of the object with the result that the latter may perform the action expressed by the lower clause.) The notion of influencing appears to be appropriate for *prevent,* at least in the case of sentences such as (1a–b), which would seem to motivate an object control analysis for *prevent.* However, given the difference in the classic analyses of Postal (1974) and Sag and Pollard (1991), it is of interest to examine the question of the grammatical analysis of *prevent* further. Neither Postal (1974) nor Sag and Pollard (1991) brought authentic corpus data to bear on the issue, but this can be done here, even if the present study cannot aspire to answer all questions that arise in the grammatical analysis of the two types of non-finite complements.

The task is to consider the question of whether corpus evidence can shed light on the grammatical analysis of the NP *from -ing* and NP *-ing* complements of *prevent*. The NOW Corpus may be consulted first, and this is followed with a consultation of the Hansard Corpus and COHA, to shed further light on the recent history of the two constructional variants. A suitable way to approach the question of the grammatical properties of the complements of *prevent*—regarding the relevance of NP Movement or object control—is to consider special NPs, especially existential *there*, that can be used as standard tests to distinguish object control from NP Movement, or from Subject to Object Raising in this case. The term "Subject to Object Raising" may be felt to be dated, but it is a richly descriptive label for the rule and it can be used for ease of reference to designate the specific type of NP Movement in question. Existential *there* is restricted to a very limited set of predicates, and it tends to be disallowed as the object argument of an object control verb. For instance, we may compare *John expected there to be trouble at the meeting*, where *expect* is a Subject to Object Raising verb and *there* is raised from the lower clause, with **John persuaded there to be trouble at the meeting*, which is unlikely because the object control verb *persuade* cannot assign a theta role to the special NP *there*.

Turning to the NOW Corpus, the simple search string "[prevent].[v*] there" appears suitable to gain information on the two constructions with *there* as the post-verbal NP. The search string retrieves 43 tokens from the entire NOW Corpus. Of these ten are irrelevant and need to be excluded. Two examples are given in (6a–b).

(6) a. So far that's 12 million abortions the Population Fund has pre-vented there. (NOW, IE, 2017, *Irish Times*)
   b. If a forest fire cannot be prevented there are tools to combat the blaze. (NOW, CA, 2012, *Net Newsledger*)

In neither of (6a–b) does *there* depend on *prevent*, and such tokens can be set aside. The remaining 31 tokens are relevant to the present investigation. Perhaps somewhat surprisingly, the great majority of them, 24 in all, are of the NP *-ing* type, and only 7 are of the NP *from -ing* type. Two illustrations of each type are given in (7a–b) and (8a–b).

(7) a. A central database for the state to track those who were arrested and convicted of domestic violence, perhaps preventing there from being future victims. (NOW, US, 2017, WAAY)
   b. It is the last substantial strip left which prevents there from being an urban sprawl from London to Crawley […] (NOW, GB, 2010, Telegraph.co.uk)

(8) a. Scottish Labour MSP Neil Findlay, who convenes the Scottish Parliament's Health and Sport Committee, said the two patients had participated in the review in good faith "to prevent there being further victims." (NOW, GB, 2017, Holyrood.com)
   b. You would prevent there being a person in charge just because of that. (NOW, US, 2010, CNN Political Ticker)

As regards the spread of the 24 tokens of the NP -*ing* type, 10 of them are from British English, five from Australian, three from Malaysian English, and two from American English. The remaining tokens are single tokens from a range of geographical areas, including Canada and India. As for the 7 tokens of the NP *from* -*ing* type, four of these are from American English, with one each from British, Australian and New Zealand English.

It was observed in Sect. 6.2 that in each of the five regional varieties that are the main focus of this investigation the NP *from* -*ing* type of complement is considerably more frequent than the NP -*ing* type. In the light of that finding the results emerging from the examination of the *there* test, showing that in this context, the reverse is true, are surprising, and worth investigating further. British English turned out to yield the most tokens with respect to the pattern where *prevent* is followed by *there*, and it is then fortunate that it is possible to shed further light on the *there* construction by considering the Hansard Corpus.

To turn to the Hansard Corpus, the search string "[prevent].[v*] there" retrieves 172 tokens and almost all of them are relevant. Exceptions include (9a–b).

(9) a. Of these, 1233 have tried to re-engage at Chingwangtao, and have been prevented there; 222 have tried to re-engage at Chifu, and have been prevented there: of the balance of 500, a number, estimated at 00, have succeeded in making their way back to the Rand: […] (Hansard, House of Commons, Feb. 23, 1906)

b. [...] but if crime is to be prevented there must be enough police patrolling the streets: [...] (Hansard, House of Commons, July 3, 2000)

As for the tokens that are relevant to this investigation in Hansard, there are only one or two prior to the 1870s, but from then on, more substantive numbers of tokens are encountered. The numbers of tokens are given in Table 6.4.

Sentence (10) is the one example of the construction with *from*, from 2002, and three illustrations of the construction without *from* selected from different decades are given in (11a–c).

(10) As I warned last week, we must not let divisions among those who want reform to [*sic*] prevent there from being any reform. (Hansard Corpus, House of Lords, Jan. 15, 2002)

(11) a. LORD ESLINGTON observed, that there was nothing in the clause which would prevent there being two or three assessors, [...] (Hansard, House of Commons, June 21, 1875)

b. I hope what I have said now will prevent there being any misapprehension of what may be called the preliminary discussion [...] (Hansard, House of Commons, June 10, 1937)

Table 6.4 Non-finite complements of *prevent* with existential *there* from the 1870s to the 2000s in the Hansard Corpus

Decade	there from -ing	there -ing
1870s	0	8
1880s	0	7
1890s	0	6
1900s	0	10
1910s	0	15
1920s	0	5
1930s	0	13
1940s	0	14
1950s	0	12
1960s	0	22
1970s	0	15
1980s	0	17
1990s	0	9
2000s	1	5

c. [...] income deficiencies may prevent there being adequate
demand for the goods and services in question. (Hansard,
House of Lords, Feb. 7, 1990)

The results given in Table 6.4 testify to a very lop-sided picture regarding
the incidence of the two non-finite constructions in Hansard. In most
decades since the 1870s noticeable numbers of tokens are found of *prevent*
selecting the *there -ing* pattern, but the prepositional construction is
absent from all the decades, with the exception of one token in the 2000s.
The data from Hansard thus reinforce the finding suggested by the NOW
data that the *there* construction, often taken to be a diagnostic of NP
Movement configurations, has been much more frequent with the NP
-ing pattern than with the NP *from -ing* pattern.[4]

The question that arises from the discussion of existential *there* is
whether further information on the grammar of the two types of non-
finite complements of *prevent* might be provided by the consideration of
other special NPs that can also be used as diagnostics of the distinction
between NP Movement (Subject to Object Raising) and object control.
Some of the special NPs commonly used are very rare and therefore
unlikely to be useful for the present purpose, including the NP *cognizance*
found as an idiom chunk in the idiom *take cognizance of*. However, the NP
advantage, found in the idiom *take advantage of*, is more promising. The
search string "[prevent].[v*] advantage" does in fact produce 14 tokens in
Hansard. Of these, 12 are of the NP *-ing* type without *from*, and two are
of the NP *from -ing* type. The two tokens of the latter type are given in
(12a–b), and two examples of the type without *from* are given in (13a–b).

(12) a. The provisions have been so drawn as to prevent advantage
from being taken of this simplification to the detriment of
either the Revenue or of trade competitors [...] (Hansard,
House of Commons, May 7, 1957)

b. My main reason for intervening in this debate is to emphasize
the fact of the poverty in Hong Kong, which prevents advantage from being taken not only of primary education, but still
more of secondary education facilities [...] (Hansard, House of
Lords, Dec. 19, 1967)

(13) a. [...] it was thought necessary to prevent advantage being taken
of technical inaccuracies in carrying out their novel enactments.
(Hansard, House of Commons, May 10, 1875)

b. That needs to be coupled with a direction to arbitrators in rent
reviews to prevent advantage being taken of the new situation
in the context of rent reviews on agricultural tenancies [...]
(Hansard, House of Lords, Oct. 18, 1993)

The example in (13a) is the earliest of the 12 tokens of the construction
without *from*, and as regards the other tokens of this type, they include
one from 1895 and 1917 and two each from the 1930s and the 1940s,
again one from 1954 and 1964, with a further two from the 1970s. For
their part, the tokens with the preposition are 1957 and 1967, as spelled
out in (12a–b). It is hardly possible to speak of clustering with only two
tokens, but the fact that both were found in fairly recent English might
still be suggestive that the construction with *from* in the case of special
NPs—those that are diagnostic of Subject to Object Raising—might be in
its very first incipient stage, at least in this text type of British English.[5]
Here it is also recalled that the one token of the construction with *from*
involving *there* was from 2002.

One possible conclusion suggested by the differences in usage found in
the NOW Corpus and in Hansard is that the fairly easy availability of constructions consisting of *there -ing* with *prevent* indicates that the construction without the preposition is more amenable to analysis as a Subject to
Object Raising construction than the construction with the preposition.
The findings relating to the NP *advantage* are in line with this conclusion.
A possible approach would be to view *prevent* as straddling the divide
between NP Movement and object control, in permitting both types of
constructions, with the proviso that in the case of the variant with the
preposition the NP Movement construction is only in its incipient stages.

As for the construction without the preposition, it is not in fact clear to
the present investigators whether tokens of the type of (11a–c) should
necessarily always be analyzed as involving NP Movement during all periods of recent English. That is, it is possible that such sentences, and non-
finite constructions selected by *prevent* without the preposition *from* more
generally, may involve, or may have involved, neither object control nor
NP Movement. A conceivable possibility is that the string NP -*ing* selected
by *prevent* may be, or may have been, a clausal complement of the type
postulated by Postal (1974, 104–105) for verbs such as *resent*. The construction might be called *Acc -ing*, to use a term from Ross (2004), with
the NP that follows *prevent* not being raised by Subject to Object Raising,
but instead remaining in situ as the subject of the lower clause (but still in

an oblique form). As Postal noted, for verbs of the *resent* class the lower subject is not raised, and a sentence such as *They resented it happening to Bob* does not permit *It was resented happening to Bob* (the latter sentence from Postal 1974, note 16). Similarly, a passive of the type *There may be prevented by income deficiencies being adequate demand for the goods and services in question*, as a passive version of (11c), seems inconceivable. (It would remain inconceivable even if the *by* phrase were omitted.)

The special NPs may be thought to be exceptional in not permitting passive versions, but as far as constructions where the NP that follows *prevent* in the active version is a "normal" NP are concerned, scholars have also questioned the status of the passives of *prevent* lacking *from* in the complement in current English. Thus Aarts (2012) suggests that while *The sailor was prevented from drowning the cat* is well formed, the version without *from* is ill formed, i.e., *The sailor was prevented drowning the cat*. (The sentences, with the star in the second, are from Aarts 2012, 103; see also the comments in Rudanko 2003.) At the same time, Aarts (2012, 103) notes that in earlier English such constructions were well formed, pointing to two examples in the *OED*, from 1768 and 1835, respectively, and to one example with *stop* as the matrix verb, from 1895. To consider this question further, it is again of interest to consult Hansard. As regards the choice of search string, the simple string "[vb*] prevented [v?g*]" seems suitable, where the first term designates the different forms of the verb *be*. Table 6.5 gives information on the incidence of passives of *prevent* with the pattern without the preposition in the course of the last two centuries.

Three illustrations, selected from different periods of the corpus, are given in (14a–c). As was seen in Table 6.2 and examples (4c–d), the active constructions of the NP *-ing* pattern were easily found throughout the period.

(14) a. [...] he declared, that if he was prevented flogging the women, he would keep them in solitary confinement without food [...] (Hansard, House of Commons, June 1, 1824)

b. [...] Matthew Kelly, county councillor of county Clare, was prevented addressing his constituents, [...] (Hansard, House of Commons, May 10, 1901)

c. We would not want to be prevented obtaining information about a property that someone had failed to declare when making a claim for benefit [...] (Hansard, House of Lords, Feb. 1, 2001)

Table 6.5   Incidence of passive uses of *prevent* with the NP -*ing* constructions in the Hansard Corpus from the 1810s to the 2000s (pmw = per million words)

Decade	Number of tokens (pmw)
1810s	4 (0.56)
1820s	5 (0.43)
1830s	44 (1.57)
1840s	42 (1.38)
1850s	61 (1.85)
1860s	42 (1.23)
1870s	39 (1.05)
1880s	66 (1.10)
1890s	38 (0.74)
1900s	35 (0.54)
1910s	43 (0.54)
1920s	7 (0.10)
1930s	1 (0.01)
1940s	4 (0.04)
1950s	2 (0.02)
1960s	0
1970s	0
1980s	0
1990s	0
2000s	31 (0.35)

The information in Table 6.5 shows that the passive construction lacking *from* was clearly possible with *prevent* and fairly frequent in most decades of the nineteenth century. That is, the analyst should be open to the idea that the NP that follows *prevent* in active sentences, as in (4c–d), is taken to be a main clause constituent in both (14a–c) and in (4c–d).

At the same time, it should be added that the variant with *from*, while not documented in Table 6.5, was always much more frequent in the Hansard Corpus, even between 1830–1919, i.e. the period when the passive versions of the *prevent* NP -*ing* construction were most numerous. After the 1910s the use of the variant without *from* declined dramatically, and the construction became extremely rare in several decades of the twentieth century. During these decades the pattern with *from* continued to be used with a high frequency. For example, in the year 1881 alone as many as 88 relevant tokens (14.99 per million words) were found of the passive *prevent* NP *from* -*ing* construction, and 30 years later, in 1911, the number of relevant tokens of the variant with *from* was 97 (8.77 per million words). What is remarkable with respect to the construction without *from* in the Hansard Corpus is that this variant staged a dramatic comeback in the most recent decade, with the construction with *from* nevertheless continuing to be many times more frequent.[6]

An examination of the entire NOW Corpus shows that, as observed in the most recent decade of the Hansard data, tokens of the construction without *from* selected by *prevent* in the passive are attested in present-day English. Again, the tokens are most numerous in the sections representing news data from Great Britain as well as Ireland (11 and 9 tokens, respectively), but no relevant occurrences were found in the American or Philippine English sections. In the Indian and Pakistani English sections, only one relevant occurrence was found in each section.[7] Examples (15a–b) serve as illustrations:

(15) a. Nigel Farage was prevented becoming MP in Thanet when ballet boxes went missing. (NOW, GB, 2017, *Stoke Sentinel*)

b. Lawyers for convicted serial killer Mark Nash have told the Supreme Court the delay in charging him with the murders of two women in Grangegorman, Dublin, meant he was prevented making an earlier application for parole. (NOW, IR, 2016, *Irish Times*)

The hesitation of scholars about sentences of the type pointed out by Aarts (2012, 103), as in his sentence *∗The sailor was prevented drowning the cat*, is understandable in light of the rarity of the construction during most decades of the twentieth century. One general factor that may have played a role is the Complexity Principle (Rohdenburg 1996), favouring the more explicit variant with the preposition in a more complex environment. However, that principle can hardly explain the dramatic fluctuations in usage during the last hundred years, and it seems reasonable to assume that during most decades of the twentieth century, *prevent*, when selecting the complement construction without *from*, behaved like a *resent* class verb, or at least it appears that it tended to behave that way, to use the idea of gradience that has become prominent recently. During that period, the post-verbal NP tended to be interpreted as being a constituent of the lower clause. However, in very recent British English it appears that the NP may again more easily be interpreted as being in the higher clause.

The conclusion that the post-verbal NP in the NP *-ing* pattern selected by *prevent* is a constituent of the higher clause in the nineteenth century, part of the twentieth and again in very recent English brings up the question of whether the structures are derived by Subject to Object Raising or object control. The present authors do not want to insist on an "either/or" answer to this question. Subject to Object Raising was shown to have been possible for the construction without *from* by the discussion of special NPs above. As for object control, the semantic interpretation of the construction can be of the influence type, typical of object control (see Sect. 6.1), as it is in (4c–d). Indeed, in some important work on *prevent* (see especially Dixon 1991, 236–237), the NP *-ing* construction has been linked to direct influencing, which would be in line with the object control approach.

6.4   CONCLUDING REMARKS

A study of the occurrence of the two constructions in the five regional varieties of English in the NOW Corpus in Sect. 6.2 showed that British English stands out from the other varieties in allowing more readily the omission of the preposition *from*. The three non-core varieties examined in the present study, Indian, Pakistani, and Philippine English, are similar to American English in that the construction with *from* is clearly preferred. On the basis of data from the Hansard Corpus and COHA, the position of the construction *prevent* NP *-ing* in British English was stronger than it was in American English already in the nineteenth century. The influence of British English on the language patterns used in its former colonies, then, is not visible in this regard in the present day as far as Indian and Pakistani English are concerned.

Regarding our findings in Sect. 6.3, the present discussion suggests that the two non-finite complement constructions selected by *prevent* do not necessarily have the same derivational properties and that the concept of gradience needs to be invoked in their analysis. As far as the NP *from -ing* construction is concerned, it seems clear that provision needs to be made for the NP that follows *prevent* to be in the higher clause throughout the period under consideration, in view of the passivization data. Further, it seems that an object control analysis is generally to be preferred over Subject to Object Raising in the case of the prepositional pattern, because of the very low number of special NPs found in the construction in the corpora. Still, in very recent English there may be some incipient change with the construction becoming more amenable to Subject to Object Raising. As far as the NP *-ing* complement construction is concerned, the construction is much more frequent in British English than in other regional varieties, and the discussion of it here has devoted attention to that regional variety. Again, the discussion shows that in the nineteenth century and the first half of the twentieth century provision needs to be made for the NP of the pattern to be a constituent of the higher clause, because of Passivization, and it shows further that special NPs can follow *prevent* in the construction. This suggests that Subject to Object Raising should be allowed as a derivational option. At the same time, the semantics of the construction can motivate an object control analysis. Further, the dearth of passives during a 40 year period in Hansard in the second half of the twentieth century makes it plausible to assume that the construction became less amenable to Raising or object control in the course of the twentieth century, and that an *Acc -ing* analysis is also required for NP *-ing* complements of *prevent* in recent English. In very recent British English there are signs that the decline of Raising possibilities is being reversed, and that Subject to Object Raising or object control may again be in the process of becoming an option in the case of the NP *-ing* complement construction.

NOTES

1. Shastri (1996) is an early corpus-based study of complementation in Indian English, and therefore also worth noting, but it is understandably restricted because the corpora available at that time were small. For instance, the author only found one token of the "*prevent* NP *-ing*" pattern in LOB *My urgent duty now was to prevent it doing what, if left to itself, it would do* (R09 177), and hesitated about its status, but also mentioned a comment by Geoffrey Leech in a footnote (his footnote 5):

   > 5. Professor Geoffrey Leech feels that this [the sentence quoted from LOB] could be acceptable, although "prevent it *from* doing" would be more "natural" (personal communication). (Shastri 1996, 81)

2. While India and Pakistan have had historical ties with Great Britain, it is worth adding that the language policies towards English have been different in these two countries (see Schilk et al. 2012, 139–140).

3. Based on studies of the two constructions in the LOB and F-LOB corpora, Mair (2002) observes that the NP *-ing* pattern with *prevent* had been gain-

ing ground between 1961 and 1991/92. This observation is not clearly supported by the findings in the two much larger corpora examined in the present study (NOW Corpus and the Hansard Corpus), which both seem to suggest that in present-day British English, the NP *from -ing* construction is more common than the NP *-ing* construction.

4. It may be added that in COHA the corresponding search for "[prevent]. [v*]" retrieves only three relevant tokens, two from the 1860s and one from 1900. All three tokens, like the huge majority of the tokens from Hansard, are of the NP *-ing* type. An example from among the three is given in (i).

(i) The failure of the scheme, which, to use his own words, aimed at preventing there being any poor or over-rich persons in the state, entailed his disgrace and fall from power. (COHA, 1900, NF)

5. The special NP *advantage* with *prevent* does indeed seem to be more typically found in formal types of texts such as Parliamentary speeches. In the NOW Corpus, for example, the search string "[prevent].[v*] advantage" produces no occurrences in the entire 5.9-billion-word corpus, nor can the sequence be found in the 560-million-word Corpus of Contemporary American English, which represents language from different genres between 1990–2017.

6. It is worth noting that in the Hansard Corpus, the normalized frequencies of the passive versions of both variants, with and without *from*, went down in the twentieth century. However, the frequencies of the variant with the preposition *from* did not decrease in the twentieth century as dramatically as its counterpart without *from*; instead, in the passive it has consistently been much more frequent than the variant without *from*.

7. Only a handful of relevant tokens of the passive *prevent* NP *-ing* construction were found in other sections of the NOW Corpus: five tokens were found in the Sri Lankan section, three tokens in the South African, two in New Zealand, and one token each in the Australian, Hong Kong, and Nigerian sections.

The searches also produced some irrelevant hits where the *-ing* clause following *prevent* is a clausal adjunct of manner (typically with the verb *use*) rather than a complement, as in examples (ii) and (iii):

(ii) Devastating inherited diseases could be prevented using a pioneering fertility technique to swap DNA between eggs, scientists believe. (NOW, GB, 2010, *Independent*)

(iii) In most treatments, the tumor is first removed and a re-occurrence is prevented using local radiation therapy or chemotherapy, followed by hormone therapy. (NOW, IN, 2017, *The Asian Age*)

It is perhaps worth noting that in cases comparable to those in (ii–iii), the *-ing* clause is headed by the preposition *by*. One can of course contemplate whether the existence of instances such as (ii–iii) might partly explain why the relevant passives of *prevent* NP *-ing* are not more numerous; however, considering that the frequencies of tokens similar to (ii–iii) are also rather low, it is unlikely that they would have an effect on the matter.

REFERENCES

Aarts, Bas. 2012. *Small Clauses in English: The Nonverbal Types.* Berlin and Boston: De Gruyter, Inc. Accessed 23 March 2018. ProQuest Ebook Central.

Bernaisch, Tobias, Stefan Th. Gries, and Joybrato Mukherjee. 2014. The Dative Alternation in South Asian English(es). *English World-Wide* 35 (1): 7–31.

Carnie, Andrew. 2007. *Syntax. A Generative Introduction.* 2nd ed. Malden, MA: Blackwell.

Deshors, Sandra C. 2015. A Multifactorial Approach to Gerundial and *to*-infinitival Verb-Complementation Patterns in Native and Non-Native English. *English Text Construction* 8 (2): 207–235. https://doi.org/10.1075/etc.8.2.04des.

Deshors, Sandra C., and Stefan Th. Gries. 2016. Profiling Verb Complementation Constructions Across New Englishes: A Two-Step Random Forests Analysis of *ing* vs. *to* Complements. *International Journal of Corpus Linguistics* 21 (2): 192–218. https://doi.org/10.1075/ijcl.21.2.03des.

Dixon, R.M.W. 1991. *A New Approach to English Grammar, on Semantic Principles.* Oxford: Clarendon Press.

Huddleston, Rodney, and Geoffrey K. Pullum. 2002. *The Cambridge Grammar of the English Language.* Cambridge: Cambridge University Press.

Mair, Christian. 2002. Three Changing Patterns of Verb Complementation in Late Modern English: A Real-Time Study Based on Matching Text Corpora. *English Language and Linguistics* 6 (1): 105–131.

———. 2009. Infinitival and Gerundial Complements. In *Comparative Studies in Australian and New Zealand English – Grammar and Beyond*, ed. Pam Peters, Peter Collins, and Adam Smith, 261–274. Amsterdam: John Benjamins.

Mair, Christian, and Geoffrey Leech. 2006. Current Changes in English Syntax. In *The Handbook of English Linguistics*, ed. B. Aarts and A. McMahon, 328–342. Malden, MA: Wiley-Blackwell.

Mukherjee, Joybrato. 2003. The Lexicogrammar of Present-Day Indian English. In *Exploring the Lexis-Grammar Interface*, ed. Ute Romer and Rainer Schulz, 117–135. Amsterdam: John Benjamins.

Mukherjee, Joybrato, and Sebastian Hoffmann. 2006. Describing Verb-Complementational Profiles of New Englishes. *English Word-Wide* 27: 147–173.

Mukherjee, Joybrato, and Marco Schilk. 2008. Verb-Complementational Profiles Across Varieties of English: Comparing Verb Classes in Indian English and

British English. In *The Dynamics of Linguistic Variation: Corpus Evidence on English Past and Present*, ed. Terttu Nevalainen, Irma Taavitsainen, Päivi Pahta, and Minna Korhonen, 163–181. Amsterdam: John Benjamins.

Postal, Paul M. 1974. *On Raising: One Rule of English Grammar and Its Theoretical Implications*. Cambridge, MA: MIT Press.

Radford, Andrew. 1981. *Transformational Syntax*. Cambridge: Cambridge University Press.

Rohdenburg, Günter. 1996. The Complexity Principle as a Factor Determining Grammatical Variation and Change in English. In *Language Use, Language Acquisition and Language History: (Mostly) Empirical Studies in Honour of Rüdiger Zimmermann*, ed. Ingo Plag and Klaus Peter Schneider, 25–44. Trier: Wissenschaftlicher Verlag.

Ross, John R. 2004. Nouniness. In *Fuzzy Grammar*, ed. B. Aarts, D. Denison, E. Keizer, and G. Popova, 351–422. Oxford: Oxford University Press.

Rudanko, Juhani. 2003. Comparing Alternate Complements of Object Control Verbs: Evidence from the Bank of English Corpus. In *Corpus Analysis: Language Structure and Language Use*, ed. Pepi Leistyna and Charles F. Meyer, 273–283. Amsterdam: Rodopi.

Sag, Ivan, and Carl Pollard. 1991. An integrated Theory of Complement Control. *Language* 67: 63–113.

Schilk, Marco, Tobias Bernaisch, and Joybrato Mukherjee. 2012. Mapping Unity and Diversity in South Asian Lexicogrammar. In *Mapping Unity and Diversity World-Wide*, ed. Marianne Hundt and Ulrike Gut, 137–165. Amsterdam: John Benjamins.

Schilk, Marco, Joybrato Mukherjee, Christopher Nam, and Sach Mukherjee. 2013. Complementation of Ditransitive Verbs in South Asian Englishes: A Multifactorial Analysis. *Corpus Linguistics and Linguistic Theory* 9 (2): 187–225.

Shastri, S.V. 1996. Using Computer Corpora in the Description of Language with Special Reference to Complementation in Indian English. In *South Asian English: Structure, Use, and Users*, ed. R. Baumgardner, 70–81. Urbana: University of Illinois Press.

The Oxford English Dictionary (OED Online). 2018. Oxford: Oxford University Press. http://www.oed.com.

CHAPTER 7

Conclusion

Abstract This chapter presents an overview of the main findings and observations made in the case studies included in this book and draws attention to the methodological and theoretical considerations that are relevant to assessing the contributions of the studies to the broader knowledge on the variation of non-finite complement constructions in English. It is noted how diachronic and synchronic variation was seen in connection with different complement patterns with the help of large electronic corpora, and that both quantitative and qualitative analyses were applied to perceive not only the degrees of variation, but also factors potentially affecting the choice between constructions which are very similar in many respects. As regards the differences between complement constructions, evidence was found with some of the matrix predicates that supports the recently formulated Choice Principle with regard to the selection of infinitival and gerundial complements. The chapter also discusses the importance of balancing between quantitative and qualitative approaches, serving as the guiding principles of the studies in the present volume, and looks ahead to the possible avenues of further research.

Keywords Complementation • Corpus linguistics • Control • Choice principle • Regional variation

© The Author(s) 2019
M. Kaunisto, J. Rudanko, *Variation in Non-finite Constructions in English*, https://doi.org/10.1007/978-3-030-19044-6_7

This book presents a selection of studies dealing with questions on the complementation of English verbs and adjectives, with a view to exploring factors which bear on the variation attested in their use. Different types of variation are investigated with the help of diachronic as well as present-day English corpora. There are some common threads in the perspectives into the studies presented in Chaps. 2, 3, 4, 5, and 6 that deserve to be singled out, and it is hoped that the studies add to our knowledge of these issues. In addition, it is perhaps useful to reflect on the materials and methods used in the studies with regard to the findings, in order to comment on the overall aim of the present book and to contemplate the prospects of further studies.

To begin with, the patterns examined involve sentential complements with which variation has been frequently observed. There are obviously other types of complementation which are also worth investigating but which go beyond the scope of the present volume. Secondly, the studies aim to contribute to the research relating to alternation involving control, with Chaps. 2, 3, and 4 focusing on constructions involving subject control, and Chaps. 5 and 6 focusing on constructions involving object control. Many of the constructions also have a sentential complement headed by a preposition; in some of the patterns the variation occurs between the use of two prepositions, or the use or non-use of a single preposition.

Electronic corpora feature prominently throughout the volume as a main source of data. Instances of authentic occurrences were regarded as instrumental not only as regards quantifying degrees of use and variation of different constructions, but qualitative observations were also frequently made on relevant tokens with regard to semantic and pragmatic considerations in the use of the constructions. It almost goes without saying that especially when it comes to the study of individual matrix predicates, corpora need to have a large word count in order to provide scholars with sufficient numbers of tokens to examine, and for the present volume several diachronic and present-day English corpora were examined. In this regard, we are naturally very grateful to the work by all the people involved in the compilation of these resources. Until fairly recently, the largest available corpora typically represented the main varieties of English, i.e., American and British English, but now large, representative corpora including data of Outer Circle varieties of English are making it possible to cast the net wider to examine patterns of complementation also in some of these varieties, which is another aim present in Chaps. 5 and 6.

As regards tracing diachronic changes in the use of the "rival" complement patterns across the last couple of centuries in the history of the
English language, the two main corpora representing American and British
English used in the studies here—COHA and the Hansard Corpus—were
usually helpful for the purpose of detecting major changes in the overall
degrees of use of the patterns. In cases involving variation between infinitival and gerundial complement patterns—as seen in connection with the
matrix predicates *frightened* and *submit*—the nineteenth century data
shows a general preference towards infinitival complements while the
gerundial complements began to increase in frequency in the twentieth
century. The increase in the use of gerundial complements is in line with
the overall diachronic changes in the system of English complementation,
now often referred to as the Great Complement Shift. Major overall shifts
in preference were also seen in connection with variation of other types of
complement patterns: for example, of the two gerundial constructions
selected by *work*, headed by different prepositions (*at* and *on*), the *at -ing*
pattern was clearly observed as having been more frequent in the nineteenth century, while tokens of *work on -ing* increased in frequency in the
late twentieth century. Similarly, two object control patterns selected by
the matrix predicates *warn* and *prevent* showed diachronic variation
between patterns with either overt or covert NP objects (*warn* (NP)
against -ing) or patterns where the head preposition of the gerundial complement is omissible (*prevent* NP (*from*) *-ing*).

However, the main focus in the case studies was on the nature of variation in recent English, and with close analysis of larger amounts of data it
has been possible to find differences in the uses of the patterns, which
supports Bolinger's (1968) idea that syntactic differences of structures
tend to be indicative of semantic or pragmatic differences. The case studies
involved examining the complement patterns from a number of different
theoretical perspectives. The significance of the Choice Principle, formulated in Rudanko (2017), was examined in connection with the variation
between complement patterns selected by the matrix predicates *frightened*
and *submit* (examined in Chaps. 3 and 4, respectively). The principle predicts infinitival complements to be more closely associated with agentive,
[+Choice] contexts while gerunds tend to be used in non-agentive, [−
Choice] contexts. In the case of both *frightened* and *submit*, it seems that
this type of difference may indeed be an influencing factor in the choice of
the complement pattern. This seems to hold particularly in cases in which
the lower clauses are in the passive, i.e. contexts which would be

prototypically [–Choice], as the large majority of the tokens of this type found in present-day data had gerundial complements. It is important to note that the matrix predicates and their complements in the active voice do allow some flexibility in this regard, and the condition is by no means categorical—however, the tendency reached statistical significance. It was furthermore interesting to observe that the tendency seemed to be stronger in present-day American English than in British English, and the possible spread of this feature into other regional varieties of English may be worth studying in greater detail in the future. While it has been established that there are many factors that play a role in the selection between infinitival and gerundial complements, the findings here in relation to the Choice Principle seem to warrant further study in connection with other matrix predicates.

The analyses of corpus data in connection with the matrix predicates have also given rise to other kinds of theoretical considerations. As regards the patterns *work at -ing* and *work on -ing*, examined in Chap. 2, it was proposed that while there is semantic overlap between the two constructions, differences perceived in their use may reflect the fundamental meanings of the prepositions *at* and *on* themselves. As regards the matrix verb *submit* (Chap. 4), in addition to observing the influence of the Choice Principle, it was noted that in present-day English the *to* infinitive has become rarer than the *to -ing* complement pattern. It was proposed that perhaps some of the diachronic developments in the variation between infinitival and gerundial complement patterns may have been due to changes in the interpretation of the status of *to* in *to* infinitives as an auxiliary or a preposition, for which supplementary evidence was found in diachronic corpus data. In other words, the reason for the increase of the *to -ing* pattern may have been a grammar internal one.

The possible semantic and pragmatic factors influencing the variation between overt and covert object NP patterns in the case of *warn* (NP) *against -ing* were discussed in Chap. 5. In present-day English, the object is omissible, as in *They warned against drawing conclusions hastily.* Such instances are of interest as they go against Bach's Generalization, according to which noun phrase objects cannot be omitted in object control structures. The tokens were analysed in terms of whether the lower level predicate involved a sense of regularity or habituality, or whether the action denoted by the predicate was actualized or not. It was observed that an irrealis interpretation was relevant for the lower level predicates in most of the instances. Another factor considered had to do with the specificity of the understood object, and some instances were particularly interesting in that there was a degree of indeterminacy in the interpretations of the understood object, and it was proposed, along the lines as suggested in Rudanko and Rickman (2014), that there might, in fact, be certain circumstances in which it may be politic or less face-threatening not to specify the identity of the understood object, which in this construction is coreferential with the subject of the lower predicate. This type of analysis could also be extended in the future to other semantically similar object control matrix verbs.

The complement constructions in Chap. 6 involve the object control verb *prevent* and the omissibility of the preposition *from* (i.e. *prevent* NP (*from*) *-ing*), as in *The accident prevented him bowling*, which has been observed as being typically found in British English. In addition to examining the frequencies of use of the constructions with or without the preposition in different regional varieties of English, the question of the derivation of the constructions was raised as a relevant issue when describing the variation between the patterns. It was noted that there are grounds to regard the post-verbal NP as belonging to the main clause, and that at least in the NP *from -ing* construction, *prevent* has been analyzed as an NP Movement or Subject to Object Raising verb. On the other hand, *prevent* has also been listed in earlier studies as an object control verb, an interpretation of which seems very relevant in cases where the referent of the subject influences the action of the referent of the object. Some standard tests used to distinguish object control and NP Movement were applied in the formulation of corpus queries, such as the compatibility of the verb with existential *there*, which is associated with Subject to Object Raising verbs. The majority of the tokens found of the constructions in the corpus with existential *there* were of the "NP *-ing*" type, which is noteworthy because in general the "NP *from -ing*" pattern is considerably more common than the construction without the preposition, even in British English. Based on similar tokens in the Hansard Corpus, the "NP *-ing*" pattern has clearly been the preferred form with existential *there* in the last two centuries, and from the viewpoint of diagnostic tests of NP Movement, the *there* construction clearly seems to favour "NP *-ing*" pattern. Further corpus data was also examined of instances of *prevent* in the passive. Overall, based on the findings of the constructions in specific test patterns, it seems that the two constructions selected by *prevent* may have different derivational properties, with the prepositional pattern favouring an object control analysis since very few instances of existential *there* were found with this construction, while the occurrence of "NP -*ing*" with special NPs and passivization in earlier times and again in very recent English suggests that the "NP -*ing*" construction may be derived by NP Movement, although semantic aspects of the construction also invite at least the possibility of an object control analysis. The fluctuation and changing trends in the corpus data make *prevent* an interesting verb in this respect, and there is scope for further research.

As has been noted, the case studies have involved both qualitative and quantitative approaches to the study of the variation in the use of non-finite complement constructions, and a number of potential influencing factors and descriptions of the grammatical structures have been discussed. In addition to referring to frequencies of tokens, close manual inspection of the data has also played an important role. Where the categories used allowed quantification, calculations were made of the statistical significance of the findings. In many cases, the perceived tendencies have been numerically fairly clear-cut and the corresponding Chi Square values further confirm the findings. It is perhaps worth pointing out that the statistical analyses in the case studies were conducted to serve the immediate purpose of, for example, determining the association between infinitival and gerundial patterns and [+Choice] or [−Choice] contexts. In recent studies on variation in complementation, more sophisticated statistical tools have been called for and introduced, such as multifactorial regression analyses which allow the examination of the significance of multiple parameters on the choice between complement patterns (see e.g. De Smet 2013; Deshors 2015; Deshors and Gries 2016). Such studies have typically not focused on individual matrix predicates but on variation between complement patterns on the whole. As stated in the introductory chapter, however, the approach adopted here in which individual matrix predicates are examined separately in detail enables the observation of more subtle differences, and surveying the variation between individual case studies can then be used for making broader generalizations.

Applying regression analyses to case studies such as the ones presented in this book is undoubtedly an avenue worth exploring. Obviously, this requires even larger sets of data than the ones analysed here, and with the low frequencies of some individual matrix predicates, attempting to examine the proportional weight of different factors might lead to unreliable results. Considering the theoretical questions raised in the case studies, this has also not been one of the main points of interest. Furthermore, the present authors would rather caution against trying to portray some of the suggested factors potentially influencing the choice of the complement patterns as ones that are easily identifiable or categorizable. For example, the degrees of specificity of understood noun phrase objects, raised in connection with the construction *warn* (NP) *against -ing*, probably have to do with a notion that is too diffuse to permit clear and unequivocal boundaries between categories such as specific, indeterminate or general. From this point of view, it is perhaps preferable to first examine the overall question in greater detail. As for Chap. 3, it might seem at first sight that a binary logistic regression analysis would be attractive with respect to the relevance of extractions and of the Choice Principle since the contexts are analyzed as [+/−Extraction] and the lower predicates are analyzed as [+/−Choice]. However, the number of extraction contexts turns out to be so small—for instance, only 9 in the case of some 200 tokens in the data from COCA—that it makes better sense to exclude them from further analysis, and instead to highlight the statistical significance of the Choice Principle in the present data.

The corpora examined in the case studies provide a broad range of different types of authentic usage of language in terms of temporal and stylistic differences of written and spoken data. However, it is useful to remind the reader that because of the differences in the principles followed when the corpora were compiled and composed, the corpus findings may reflect different kinds of things about the language use of a given regional variety or register at any particular point of time. In other words, the results gleaned from the BNC, representing mostly British English around the late 1980s and early 1990s, are likely to reflect quite a different type of overall language use than the results from the same period in the Hansard Corpus. Instead of seeing this as a hindrance, it could be argued that it is the task and responsibility of the scholar to interpret the results when the data is compositionally heterogeneous. At the same time, new corpora are being compiled and made available to linguists. In the case studies of this book, a number of different corpora have deliberately been used in order to serve the purposes of finding out further details about the use of the complementation patterns under examination. In the case of some studies, individual corpora may have been consulted for a specific narrow purpose (for example, in Chap. 4 instances of post-auxiliary ellipsis with a number of selected verbs were examined in the CLMET3.0 corpus). The two large corpora including data from Inner as well as Outer Circle varieties of English, the GloWbE corpus and the more recent NOW corpus, have made it possible to extend the study of individual matrix predicates from the major varieties to other regional varieties. The two corpora pose their own challenges to the linguist, and some concerns have been voiced as regards their representativeness of different regional varieties (see e.g. Hoffmann 2018 on the GloWbE corpus), but the present authors nevertheless find that the corpora offer interesting data on the relationship between the usage in core and ESL varieties. In Chaps. 5 and 6, comparisons were made between American and British English and three Asian varieties of English, of which Indian and Pakistani English might have been expected to show similarities with British English as regards the use of complementation patterns, because of historical and administrative ties between the countries. However, all of the three Asian varieties turned out to be more similar to usage patterns in American English. The options and prospects for further study, both in terms of the number of varieties and registers—as well as the matrix predicates and their complementation patterns—are rich and promising.

REFERENCES

Bolinger, Dwight. 1968. Entailment and the Meaning of Structures. *Glossa* 2: 119–127.

De Smet, Hendrik. 2013. *Spreading Patterns: Diffusional Change in the English System of Complementation*. Oxford: Oxford University Press.

Deshors, Sandra C. 2015. A Multifactorial Approach to Gerundial and *to*-infinitival Verb-Complementation Patterns in Native and Non-Native English. *English Text Construction* 8 (2): 207–235. https://doi.org/10.1075/etc.8.2.04des.

Deshors, Sandra C., and Stefan Th. Gries. 2016. Profiling Verb Complementation Constructions Across New Englishes: A Two-Step Random Forests Analysis of *ing* vs. *to* Complements. *International Journal of Corpus Linguistics* 21 (2): 192–218. https://doi.org/10.1075/ijcl.21.2.03des.

Hoffmann, Sebastian. 2018. I Would Like to Request for Your Attention: On the Diachrony of Prepositional Verbs in Singapore English. In *Changing Structures: Studies in Complementation and Constructions*, ed. Mark Kaunisto, Mikko Höglund, and Paul Rickman, 171–196. Amsterdam: John Benjamins. https://doi.org/10.1075/slcs.195.10hof.

Rudanko, Juhani. 2017. *Infinitives and Gerunds in Recent English: Studies on Non-Finite Complements in Recent English*. London: Palgrave Macmillan.

Rudanko, Juhani, and Paul Rickman. 2014. Null Objects and Sentential Complements, with Evidence from the Corpus of Historical American English. In *Corpus Interrogation and Grammatical Patterns*, ed. K. Davidse, C. Gentens, L. Ghesquière, and L. Vandelanotte, 209–221. Amsterdam: John Benjamins.

Name Index[1]

[1] Note: Page numbers followed by 'n' refer to notes.

© The Author(s) 2019
M. Kaunisto, J. Rudanko, *Variation in Non-finite Constructions in English*, https://doi.org/10.1007/978-3-030-19044-6

Subject Index[1]

A

Agentivity, 10, 40, 48, 51, 116, 133

B

Bach's Generalization, 6, 7, 82–101, 134

Bolinger's Generalization, 4, 9, 17, 40

British National Corpus (BNC), 5, 6, 8, 21, 22, 27, 32, 33, 40, 52–55, 57, 58n3, 137

C

Choice Principle, 10, 40, 47, 50–57, 71, 72, 77, 133, 134, 137

Collins COBUILD Advanced Learner's Dictionary, 23, 24, 26, 27

Complexity Principle, 108, 124

Concealed passives, 66, 69, 70, 77, 78n1

Control

object control, 5, 6, 10, 83–85, 92–96, 99, 102n2, 115–117, 120, 121, 125, 126, 132–136

subject control, 5, 16, 47, 51, 53, 62, 63, 65, 74, 77, 115, 132

Corpus of American Soap Operas (SOAP), 8, 20, 52

Corpus of Contemporary American English (COCA), 3, 8, 40, 45–54, 57, 58n2, 83, 85, 101n1, 127n5, 137

Corpus of Historical American English (COHA), 8, 9, 11, 12, 16–24, 29–31, 33, 38, 40–43, 45, 46, 57, 62–70, 74, 76, 77, 78–79n1, 84–93, 100, 108, 113, 114, 117, 125, 127n4, 133

Corpus of Late Modern English Texts, 8, 75

Covert object, 7, 84–86, 93–101, 102n2, 102n5, 134

[1] Note: Page numbers followed by 'n' refer to notes.

GPSR Compliance
The European Union's (EU) General Product Safety Regulation (GPSR) is a set of rules that requires consumer products to be safe and our obligations to ensure this.

If you have any concerns about our products, you can contact us on

ProductSafety@springernature.com

In case Publisher is established outside the EU, the EU authorized representative is:

Springer Nature Customer Service Center GmbH
Europaplatz 3
69115 Heidelberg, Germany